MW00563708

MINDTAP
ACCELERATE:
READING

CENGAGE

Australia • Brazil • Mexico • Singapore • United Kingdom • United States

MindTap Accelerate: Reading, First Edition

Product Manager: Nancy Tran

Learning Designer: Julie Bizzotto

Manager, Content Creation: Sarah Edmonds

Content Manager: Jacqueline Czel

In House SME: Anne Alexander

Subject Matter Expert: Jenny Billings

Senior Designer: Lizz Anderson

IP Analyst: Amber Hill

Digital Delivery Lead: Nikkita Kendrick

Production vendor services: Lumina Datamatics

For product information and technology assistance, contact us at **Cengage Customer & Sales Support, 1-800-354-9706 or support.cengage.com.**

For permission to use material from this text or product, submit all requests online at **www.cengage.com/permissions.**

Student Edition:
ISBN: 978-0-357-10659-4

Cengage
20 Channel Center Street
Boston, MA 02210
USA

Cengage is a leading provider of customized learning solutions with employees residing in nearly 40 different countries and sales in more than 125 countries around the world. Find your local representative at **www.cengage.com.**

Cengage products are represented in Canada by Nelson Education, Ltd.

To learn more about Cengage platforms and services, visit **www.cengage.com**

To register or access your online learning solution or purchase materials for your course, visit **www.cengagebrain.com**

Printed at CLDPC, USA, 03-19

Contents

Mastering Reading Strategies

Review Your Understanding of the Mental Skills Required for Reading

When reading, you use multiple skills as you try to understand and analyze the concepts described in the reading. Three skills that are particularly important as you read are attitude, concentration, and memory. Your attitude includes your feelings about reading, about what you read, and about your own abilities. Concentration refers to your ability to focus your attention on the reading while limiting distraction. And memory is what allows you to store and recall information—an essential part of the reading process.

Apply Your Knowledge of the Mental Skills Required for Reading

Thinking about those skills and what you read in Unit 1 in *MindTap*, fill in the "Why is this Skill Important for Reading" block for each skill below.

Reading Skill	Why is this Skill Important for Reading?
Attitude	
Concentration	
Memory	

After you have completed that, think about strategies discussed in Unit 1 as well as some personal strategies you can use to be a successful reader. Then, fill in the "How Can This Skill Be Improved for Reading" chart to help you remember to use these techniques as you read.

Reading Skill	How Can This Skill Be Improved for Reading?
Attitude	
Concentration	
Memory	

Review Your Understanding of Paraphrasing

To help you write about things you've read, you must be able to paraphrase. When you do this, you rephrase the ideas or information in your own words; however, you are allowed to use a few words from the original text. Make sure you do not take ideas out of context or change the meaning through your retelling. Because the original idea or information was not your own, you will still need to include an in-text citation. If you do not include this, you could get in trouble for plagiarism.

Apply Your Knowledge of Paraphrasing

Read the College Success passage below. Once you feel like you have a good understanding of what you've read, try your hand at paraphrasing the most important ideas and information from below. Remember, your paraphrased content should be a shorter version of what you see here.

As a student, your success in school is directly tied to your health. Lack of sleep and exercise have been associated with lower GPAs among undergraduate students. So have alcohol use, tobacco use, gambling, and chronic health conditions (University of Minnesota, 2007).

Any health habit that undermines your success in school can also undermine your success in later life. On the other hand, you can adopt habits that sustain your well-being. One study found that people lengthened their lives an average of 14 years by adopting just four habits (Khaw and Colleagues, 2008):

1. staying tobacco-free;

2. eating more fruits and vegetables;

3. exercising regularly; and

4. drinking alcohol in moderation, if at all.

Health also hinges on a habit of exercising some tissue that lies between your ears—the organ called your brain. One path to greater health starts not with new food or a new form of exercise but with new ideas.

Consider the power of beliefs, some of which create barriers to higher levels of health: "Your health is programmed by your heredity," "Some people are just low on energy," "Healthy food doesn't taste very good," and "Over the long run, people just don't change their habits." Be willing to test these ideas and change them when it serves you.

People often misunderstand what the word *health* means. Remember that this word is similar in origin to *whole*, *hale*, *hardy*, and even *holy*. Implied in these words are qualities that most of us associate with healthy people: alertness, vitality, and vigor. Healthy people meet the demands of daily life with energy to spare. Illness or stress might slow them down for a while, but they bounce back. They know how to relax, create loving relationships, and find satisfaction in their work.

_____.

_____.

_____.

_____.

_____.

_____.

_____.

_____.

_____.

_____.

_____.

_____.

Review Your Understanding of Active Reading and the KWL Strategy

Have you ever asked yourself, "What did I just read?" after "reading" a long passage? If you are a passive reader, you are not getting the most out of your reading. Just running your eyes over words is not enough. You have to concentrate and write things down; you cannot skip words or let your mind wander. In order to understand and remember what you've read, you must read actively. As a review, here is how to do just that:

1. Identify and write down the point and purpose of the reading.

2. Underline, highlight, or circle important words or phrases.

3. Determine the meanings of unfamiliar words.

4. Outline a passage in order to understand the relationships in the information.

5. Write down questions when you're confused.

6. Complete activities—such as reading comprehension questions—that follow a chapter or passage.

7   Jot down notes in the margins.

8. Think about how you can use the information or how the information reinforces or contradicts your ideas or experiences.

9. Predict possible test questions on the material.

10. Reread and review the passage when needed.

11. Study visual aids such as graphs, charts, and diagrams until you understand them.

The KWL strategy is used to guide you through a text, such as the one that follows. First, brainstorm everything you Know (K) about a topic under the K column. Next, generate a list of what you Want to Know (W) about the topic under the W column. During or after reading, answer all of the questions in the W column; you do this under the L column.

Apply Your Knowledge of Active Reading and the KWL Strategy

The topic of the passage is the function approach to leadership. Let's start this activity with a KWL chart. Before you read the passage, fill out the K column for what you already know about the topic. If you do not know a lot about the function approach, perhaps focus on the concept of leadership instead. Then, fill out the W column.

[K] now	[W] ant to Know	[L] earned

After completing the K and W columns, read this passage from a Communications textbook. After you have read it once, go back over it using the 11 active reading strategies mentioned above. While you may not need to use all 11 strategies, try to use as many as possible to help you fully understand and annotate the passage. You will also return to the KWL chart so you can complete the L column.

Function Approach to Leadership

Suppose that your boss has asked you to lead a problem-solving team that will meet in 2 weeks. Is it possible to train yourself to be a leader in 2 weeks? Not if you believe in the trait theory! You could have a nervous breakdown trying to acquire Kirkpatrick and Locke's (1991) list of six clear-cut leadership traits: "Drive, desire to lead, honesty/integrity, self-confidence, cognitive ability, and knowledge of the business" (p. 49) and three secondary traits: "Charisma, creativity/originality, and flexibility" (p. 56). How long would it take to train yourself to be ambitious, self-confident, and creative? Thinking of leadership as a list of personality traits is counterproductive.

Instead, think of leadership as activity composed of various functions or roles (Benne & Sheats, 1948; Keyton, 1999, pp. 65–67; Sayles, 1993). The function approach claims that there are certain functions or roles that must be performed if a group is to be successful. Any time you perform one of these functions, you are the leader for that period of time.

As mentioned previously, leadership may be defined as the use of power to promote the goal accomplishment and maintenance of the group (Johnson & Johnson, 2002). In other words, the leader is a person (or persons) who performs the task and maintenance functions discussed previously in this chapter. In many groups, the appointed leader performs most of the task and maintenance functions. However, in democratic groups in which the members are committed and involved, the leadership functions or roles are shared. Because it is difficult for one person, the designated leader, to guide a group through the basic problem-solving procedure and, at the same time, to be aware of all the roles that need to be performed, another member can perform some leadership functions. For example, you may be sitting next to someone who has been trying to participate in the conversation for several minutes, but the leader and the other members are so involved in what's being said that they haven't noticed. When you say, "Carol has a point she wishes to make," you are performing gatekeeping, an important leadership function.

Review Your Understanding of the Elements of Textbooks

Textbooks include common elements, so it is important for you to be able to recognize them. Doing so will help you navigate textbooks easier and locate the information you need more efficiently. The table below is a condensed review of the most common textbook elements discussed in Unit 2.

Element	What is it?
Chapter	Main division of a textbook; determined by topic, time period, steps, or related information
Objectives	Can be learning objectives or chapter objectives; they communicate the expected goal of reading the proposed information
Key Terms	Vocabulary that may be new or difficult to the reader; definitions are provided in the chapter as you go or in a glossary
Heading	The title across the top of a page or section; denotes what information will be covered or what topic will follow
Outline	Includes the key terms, main point or idea, and additional notes about the chapter; can use this as a checklist
Study Guide	Provides hints, ideas, or techniques to prepare for a test, quiz, or exam by summarizing the important information that may appear again
Review Section/ Summary	Found at the end of a chapter, summarizes the information, facts, ideas, and key terms introduced in the chapter

Apply Your Knowledge of the Elements of a Textbook

Each image below is a common part, or element, of a textbook. Label each image using the provided key.

Answer Key
Chapter   Objectives   Key Terms   Heading
Chapter Outline   Study Guide   Review Section/Summary

6

1.

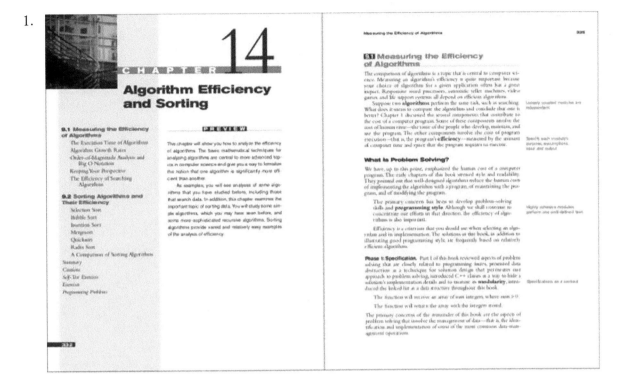

This is an example of: _____

2.

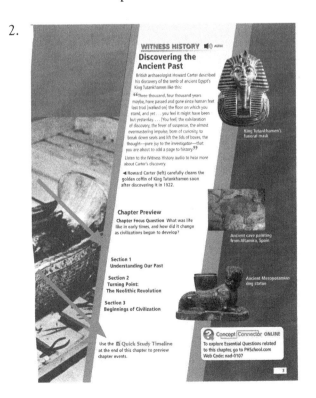

This is an example of: _____

3.

This is an example of: _____

4.

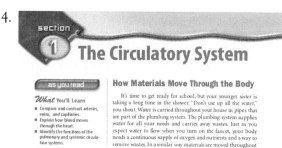

This is an example of: _____

Review Your Understanding of Other Characteristics of Textbooks

Because textbooks are written to inform, they include informative or formal language. Formal language differs from the language we use in everyday conversation; it is much more thought out, less personal, and is often used when writing for professional or academic purposes.

Type of Language	Definition
Formal	Serious, businesslike, informative, or sophisticated language
Informal	Casual or conversational, often including everyday or slang terms.

Formal language also avoids things like slang and contractions. Consider the following examples on how formal writing avoids these aspects.

Use of Slang:

Informal: The rowdy employees were acting crazy after hearing the announcement about layoffs at the factory.
Formal: The employees burst into an uproar after hearing the announcement about the layoffs at the factory.

Use of Contractions:

Informal: This essay can't be completed in a hurry.
Formal: Good essays cannot be completely quickly.

Apply Your Knowledge of Other Characteristics of Textbooks

So, where would you see formal or informal language? Consider the examples below and list whether they would include formal or informal language based on what you know about the source of information. Fill in each blank with "formal" or "informal."

1. A documentary on Netflix would include _____ language.

2. A text message conversation between two best friends would most likely include _____ language.

3. A newspaper article about coal ash in local water sources would use _____ language.

4. A new popular song on a Pop radio station would most likely utilize _____ language.

5. An emailed memo from the CEO of Amazon would include _____ language.

6. A post on a public blog or wiki could include _____ language.

7. The final draft of an essay submitted to your instructor must include _____ language.

8. The dialogue between two people in a story may include _____ language.

Considering the two items that formal writing avoids (slang and contractions), correct the following sentences. Study the informal version and locate where you can make the language more formal. Write your version on the Formal line provided.

1. Informal: The improvements aren't done until the money is handed over.

    Formal: _____

    _____

2. Informal: It was raining cats and dogs that AM.

    Formal: _____

    _____

Review Your Understanding of the Reading Strategy: REAP

The reading strategy, REAP, stands for Read-Encode-Annotate-Ponder. Following the four steps allows you to better understand, and remember, the texts you read while improving your critical thinking skills. The steps are as follows:

- Step 1: Read (carefully read the text to understand the author's ideas and information).
- Step 2: Encode (translate what you've read into your own words so you can better understand the message).
- Step 3: Annotate (to write notes or comments about a text in the margins of the text, or in a notebook, or on separate sheets of paper).
- Step 4: Ponder (reflect on what you've read and consider the thoughts of others).

Apply Your Knowledge to the Reading Strategy: REAP

Read this passage from a Biology textbook; after or while you read it, use the provided REAP diagram to consider and think critically about what you've read. Write your answers in each box provided.

The Cell Cycle

Different cells divide at different rates. Bacteria, under favorable conditions, complete a cell cycle every 20 minutes. Actively growing eukaryotic organisms might take hours, days, months, or even longer to reproduce. Nerve cells, for example, including those in the brain, might never go through cell division after they first develop.

Cell division involves two main processes, mitosis and cytokinesis. Mitosis, the process of nuclear division, ensures that each new cell receives the correct complement of chromosomes. The division of the cytoplasm to form two cells is called cytokinesis. If mitosis is not followed by cytokinesis, as occurs in some specialized skeletal muscle cells, the resulting cells become multinucleate, with more than one nucleus per cell.

The cell cycle G1 G2 includes three basic phases: interphase, mitosis, and cell division. Interphase, the growth period that follows cell division, is the phase in which the cell typically spends 90% or more of its life. If you were to view a tissue sample under a microscope, most of the cells visible would be in interphase. During interphase, the cell actively carries out all of the life processes it needs to grow, maintain itself, and function.

Interphase consists of three indistinct subphases: the phase, the S phase, and the phase. The borders between these phases are not definite. The time between the end of the previous cell division and the beginning of DNA replication is termed the phase, or first gap phase. During the phase, the cell grows and, late in this phase, synthesizes certain enzymes required for DNA synthesis.

The S phase, or synthesis phase, begins with the replication of DNA. During this time, each strand of chromatin duplicates itself, and the DNA content doubles. After it completes the S phase, the cell enters a second gap, or phase. During this time, protein synthesis increases in preparation for making enzymes needed to carry out mitosis and cytokinesis.

Cengage. "Chapter 8: How Cells Reproduce." Vital Biology for Non-Majors, 1st ed., Cengage, 2018.

R: Read	E: Encode

A: Annotate	P: Ponder

Unit 3

Building Your Word Knowledge and Vocabulary

Review Your Understanding of Look-alikes and Sound-alikes

Consider this sentence:

"**They're** eating **their** tacos over **there**."

The sentence contains three sound-alike, look-alike words: **They're** (contraction meaning *they are*), **their** (possessive pronoun meaning *belonging to them*), and **there** (an adverb meaning *in that place*). Writers commonly mix up such similar words, and by doing so they make their writing less effective — even confusing to the reader.

Remember to try these techniques to help you avoid this type of error:

1. When in doubt, use a dictionary. If you are on a computer, many search engines (Google, for instance) will define a word for you if you simply type the word followed by "define" in the search window and then hit "Enter."

    EXAMPLE: Typing "there define" in the Google search window will bring up a dictionary-style definition of the word.

2. Track sound-alike, look-alike words that you've mixed up in the past. Keep a running list and refer to it when you edit your papers.

3. Use spell-check but be mindful it won't catch all errors. For instance, a spell-check would find nothing wrong with this sentence:

    "The reins arrived in April."

    That's because "reins" means the leather straps used to steer a horse. That sentence makes sense — perhaps the reins were delivered by mail. But the author probably meant "rains" (referring to the weather).

4. Spend some time familiarizing yourself with this list of the most commonly confused words:

Word	Definition	Examples
accept	agree or receive	The candidate accepted the election results. I will accept the job offer.
except	only or excluding	I like all fruits except plums. We would go, except our car is in the repair shop.

13

Word	Definition	Examples
a lot	many or a large number of something	A lot of peanuts are grown in Virginia.
allot	to divide or share	We will allot the same amount of wall space for each child's drawings.
affect	to act on, to produce an effect	The swimmer's head cold may affect his performance in the race.
effect	result, consequence of an action	The lower prices had a positive effect on sales figures.
hear	receiving sound via the ear	I can't wait to hear that song again.
here	refers to a place, spot, or locality	I'll set your lunch down over here on the table.
its	belonging to it, possessive	Why is the computer disconnected from its power cord?
It's	a contraction for "it is"	It's a nice day out.
principal	chief or head; capital; important	The assistant principal met with the teachers before school.
principle	fundamental law or truth	"Innocent until proven guilty" is a principle of the American justice system.
than	conjunction used to show comparison between unequal items	Angela is taller than Elliot.
then	next, at that time, at same time	You tell your joke, and then I'll tell mine.
their	plural possessive pronoun	Their dog is so friendly!
they're	contraction for they are	They're on vacation in Florida.
there	in or at a place	She put your shoes in the closet over there.
to	preposition that indicates motion or direction	Let's go to the amusement park.
too	in addition, also, very	Can I go too?
two	the number after one and before three	We stayed at the snack bar for two hours.
your	possessive pronoun	I love your new shirt.
you're	contraction of you are	You're so helpful!

Apply Your Knowledge of Look-alikes and Sound-alikes

Edit these paragraphs for look-alike, sound-alike errors. Cross out any errors and write in the correct word. The first one has been done for you as an example.

Paragraph 1

They're are many common contractions in the English language, but one of those most people don't even realize is a contraction. Its a word that you probably here or say alot every day. What is the word? Its *good-bye*. Now your wondering what words make up this contraction, right? Well hear is you're answer. Good-bye is not a contraction of too words or even three words — it's a contraction of for words, and they are *God be with ye*. The word is more then 400 years old and was originally spelled as *godbwye*.

Adapted from "Good-bye." Etymonline.com, 2018, www.etymonline.com/word/good-bye#etymonline_v_9044

Paragraph 2

Did you no there is an animal called the pink fairy armadillo? This fascinating animal can control the blood flow into or out of it's distinctive pink shell. The amount of blood in the shell effects the creature's core temperature. Pink fairy armadillos are difficult too observe because there principle activity is hunting for food underground. In fact, this elusive desert-dweller is never above ground for more then a few moments at a time.

Adapted from Simon, Matt. "Absurd Creature of the Week: Pink Fairy Armadillo Crawls Out of the Desert and Into Your Heart." Wired.com, Conde Nast, 3 Jan. 2014, www.wired.com/2014/01/absurd-creature-of-the-week-pink-fairy-armadillo-crawls-out-of-the-desert-and-into-our-hearts/

Review Your Understanding of Context Clues

When you come across a word that is unfamiliar to you, keep in mind that the context around that word (the words that come before and after it, the topic of the paragraph, related images) can help you figure out the meaning.

These hints to the meaning are called **context clues**.

Here are some common types:

Context Clue Type	Description	Example
Definition	Either a direct statement of the word's meaning or a synonym of the word.	Elias is so **garrulous** that his grandmother declared him the most **talkative** person in the family. [*Garrulous* means the same as *talkative*.]
Explanation	Words, phrases, or sentences near an unfamiliar word that explain enough about that word to allow a reader to figure out its meaning.	Several species of rhinoceros are in danger of **extinction**; if we don't work to save them, they will vanish from our planet forever. [The idea that the rhinoceroses will *vanish* helps explain that *extinction* means a state of nonexistence.]
Example	An example somewhere near a word that provides an illustration allowing a reader to draw a conclusion about the word's meaning.	The villagers gathered **comestibles**, such as rice, corn, potatoes, and preserved meats. [The list of examples — rice, corn, potatoes, and preserved meats — help a reader to understand that *comestibles* means food items.]
Contrast	Nearby words, phrases, or sentences that give the opposite meaning of the unfamiliar word.	Kayla thought her manager's advice was **cryptic**, but Amanda felt it was perfectly clear. [A reader can guess that cryptic means the opposite of *clear* — *unclear* or *mysterious*.]

Apply Your Knowledge of Context Clues

Read the paragraph, and then answer the questions that follow. Do not refer to a dictionary to answer the questions.

The jolly roger is the name given to flags flown on pirate ships. Commonly a jolly roger featured a **likeness** of a skull-and-crossbones. Though sometimes the representations were of crossed swords, human skeletons, or creatures with spears. The flags were used to **intimidate** the crews of passing ships. The hope was that the crewmembers would be so scared that they would surrender to the pirates without a fight. A jolly roger flag with a black background has become **ubiquitous** in storybooks, films, and posters. In fact it is so commonly seen, that most kids can recognize it as readily as they do logos for popular brands like McDonald's and Nike. However, there is also a rarely seen version of the jolly roger with a red background. The **scarlet** background color signaled that the pirates would spare no life in a battle. While the idea of a red jolly roger may seem strange, note that the phrase *jolly roger* itself comes from the French phrase *jouli rouge* which means "pretty red."

"Rare Jolly Roger Goes on Display at Portsmouth's Navy Museum." BBC News, 14 Dec. 2011, bbc.com/news/uk-england-hampshire-16164191

1. What does **likeness** mean? _____

2. Which words or phrases near **likeness** helped you come up with the definition?

_____

3.   What does **intimidate** likely mean? _____

4.   Which words or phrases near **intimidate** helped you come up with the definition?

_____

5.   What does **ubiquitous** likely mean? _____

6.   Which words or phrases near **ubiquitous** helped you come up with the definition?

_____

7.   What does **scarlet** likely mean? _____

8.   Which words or phrases near **scarlet** helped you come up with the definition?

_____

Review Your Understanding of Word Parts and Using a Dictionary

Two other ways to determine the meaning of words are 1) using word parts, and 2) using a dictionary.

When you use word parts to determine meaning, you identify any familiar prefixes, suffixes, or word roots.

For instance, the word *uniform* contains the common prefix uni-, which means "one." The root word is *form*, which means shape or appearance. So uniform means "having one appearance." Things that are uniform look identical.

Using context clues and using word parts are both effective ways to determine the meaning of a word without interrupting the flow of your reading. However, sometimes you'll want to look up the meaning of a word in a dictionary. For instance, you may want to use a dictionary when the context doesn't hint at the meaning of the word, or if the word is used frequently in the text (like a key word), or if you are just curious to know the precise meaning.

Take a minute to review the parts of a dictionary entry. The more familiar you are with these parts, the easier it will be to learn the word and understand how to use it correctly in your own writing.

co•los•sal ◄ (kə-lŏsʹəl)

adj.

    1. Of great size, extent, or amount; immense. See Synonyms at **enermous**.
    2. Of great scope or consequence; monumental: *a colossal blunder*.

[French, from Latin colossus, *colossus*, see **colossus**.]

   co•losʹsal•ly *adv.*

Parts of a Dictionary Entry

1.	Pronunciation and syllabication	This part of the entry shows you how a word should be pronounced (or how it should sound). It will divide the word into characters or syllables.
2.	Part of speech	An abbreviation appears after the pronunciation and along with every word form. This abbreviation includes the part of speech (noun, verb, adjective, adverb, and so on).
3.	Definition	This part of the entry states the meaning of the word. Often, there is more than one meaning, and they are numbered.
4.	Examples of how the word is used	An italic phrase or a quotation that demonstrates how the word should be used.
5.	Other forms of the word	Most words have more than one form. For example, a word may be used as a noun and also as a verb or an adjective.
6.	Etymology	Information, usually in brackets, that identifies the origins and history of a word.

Apply Your Understanding of Word Parts and Using a Dictionary

Read each sentence and try to break its bolded word down into parts. See if you can identify the root word along with any prefixes and/or suffixes that are attached to it. Lastly, try to use the word's parts to come up with a definition.

Note that prefixes, suffixes and roots are usually listed in the dictionary. You may use a dictionary for this exercise.

1. The puppy's **drowsiness** got the best of him, so he lay down for a nap.

    Root: _____

    Suffix: _____

    Meaning: _____

2. This fossil **predates** dinosaurs.

    Prefix: _____

    Root: _____

    Meaning: _____

3. I just bought dark stained-glass for my bathroom; it is still **translucent**, though.

    Prefix: _____

    Root: _____

    Meaning: _____

4. Dr. Lee's **monotone** voice almost put me to sleep.

    Prefix: _____

    Root: _____

    Meaning: _____

5. The **likelihood** of winning the lottery is very low.

    Root: _____

    Suffix: _____

    Meaning: _____

Locating the Topic and Main Idea

Review Your Understanding of Determining the Topic and Main Idea

Being able to identify the topic, or subject, of a passage is critical to understanding what you read. It is also the first step in determining the main idea of a passage. The topic can be a person, place, thing, idea, or event. As we discussed in the Unit, the topic can be found in the sentence that states the main idea; it may also be repeated throughout the passage or found at the beginning or end of the passage. Because the topic can really be anywhere in the passage, it is important to know how to find it.

Once you locate the topic, figure out what the author is saying about that topic. After you have both of these, you are able to determine the main idea. Here is an example:

A *Quiet Place* was a wide release film that came out in April 2018. It grossed over 330 million dollars while in theaters. It was directed by John Krasinksi, who is known for his role in the television series *The Office*. It is a suspenseful story about a family forced to survive in a post-apocalyptic world. While the movie is classified as horror, many people classified it as sci-fi or drama.

Step 1: The topic of this paragraph is: The film *A Quiet Place*

How Do I Know? Because the entire paragraph is about the film.

Step 2: What is the Author Saying About the Topic? The author is providing information about the film and its release.

Step 3: The main idea of this paragraph is: *A Quiet Place* was a wide release film that came out in April 2018.

How Do I Know? Main ideas are often at the beginning of a paragraph. It also includes the topic. The rest of the passage speaks directly to this statement by providing more support or details.

Apply Your Knowledge of Determining the Topic and Main Idea

Read the following passage from a Sociology textbook. For each paragraph, circle the word or phrase you believe to be the paragraph's topic, then answer the questions that follow.

Deviance refers to any behavior that breaks a social norm or expectation. We often think of deviance as negative—drug use, criminal behavior, and some sexual behaviors are typically defined as deviant. But a sociological understanding of deviance also includes *positive* deviance. An exceptionally intellectually gifted person—a "genius"—would also be defined as deviant because she or he breaks the normal social expectation of intelligence.

Individuals, groups, and societies typically try to discourage deviant behavior. Sanctions are one method used to pressure people to comply with social norms and expectations. A sanction is simply the reward or punishment given to regulate behavior. The significance of the norm determines the type of reward or penalty.

1. Based on what you circled above, how did you determine the topic of paragraph one?

_____

_____

_____

_____

_____

_____

2. Based on what you circled above, how did you determine the topic of the second paragraph?

_____

_____

_____

_____

_____

3. If you had to provide a title for the passage above, what would it be and why?

_____

_____

_____

_____

_____

Now, let's practice locating the main idea of paragraphs and the larger passage as a whole. First, read the Sociology textbook excerpt below then answer the questions that follow.

Coping with Procrastination

1. Any discussion of time management would not be complete without an examination of the most well-intentioned person's worst enemy—procrastination. The dictionary (*Webster's New Collegiate*) defines *procrastination as* "the act of putting off intentionally and habitually the doing of something that should be done." Interestingly, most procrastinators do not feel that they are acting intentionally. On the contrary, they feel that they fully *intend* to do whatever it is, but they simply cannot, will not, or—bottom line—they *do not* do it. Procrastinators usually have good reasons for their procrastination (some would call them excuses): "didn't have time," "didn't feel well," "couldn't figure out what to do," "couldn't find what I needed," "the weather was too bad"—the list is never-ending.

2. Even procrastinators themselves know that the surface reasons for their procrastination are, for the most part, not valid. When procrastination becomes extreme, it is a self-destructive course, and, yet, people feel that they are powerless to stop it. This perception can become reality if the underlying cause is not uncovered. Experts have identified some of the serious underlying causes of procrastination. Think about them the next time you find yourself struck by this problem.

3. Often procrastination stems from a real or imagined fear or worry that is focused not so much on the thing you are avoiding but its potential consequences. For instance, your procrastination over preparing for an oral presentation could be based on your fear that no matter how well prepared you are, you will be overcome by nerves and forget whatever you are prepared to say. Every time you think about working on the speech, you become so worried about doing "a bad job" that you have to put the whole thing out of your mind to calm down. You decide that you will feel calmer about it tomorrow and will be in a much better frame of mind to tackle it. Tomorrow the scenario gets repeated. The best way to relieve your anxiety would be to dig in and prepare so well that you can't possibly do poorly.

4. Being a perfectionist is one of the main traits that spawns fear and anxiety. Whose expectations are we afraid of not meeting? Often it is our own harsh judgment of ourselves that creates the problem. We set standards that are too high and then judge ourselves too critically. When you picture yourself speaking before a group, are you thinking about how nervous the other students will be as well, or are you comparing your speaking abilities to the anchorperson on the six o'clock news? A more calming thought is to recall how athletes measure improvements in their performances by tracking and trying to improve on their own "personal best." Champions have to work on beating themselves in order to become capable of competing against their opponents. Concentrating on improving your own past performance, and thinking of specific ways to do so, relieves performance anxiety.

5. On the surface this would seem to be the reason for all procrastination, and the obvious answer is for the procrastinator to find a way to "get motivated." There are situations where lack of motivation is an indicator that you have taken a wrong turn. When you seriously do not want to do the things you need to do, you may need to reevaluate your situation. Did you

decide to get a degree in Information Systems because everyone says that's where the high paying jobs are going to be, when you really want to be a social worker or a travel agent? If so, when you find yourself shooting hoops or watching television when you should be putting in time at the computer lab, it may be time to reexamine your decision. Setting out to accomplish something difficult when your heart isn't in it is often the root cause of self-destructive behavior.

6. Often procrastination is due to an inability to concentrate or a feeling of being overwhelmed and indecisive. Although everyone experiences these feelings during a particular stressful day or week, a continuation of these feelings could indicate that you are in a state of burnout. Burnout is a serious problem that occurs when you have overextended yourself for too long a period of time. It is especially likely to occur if you are pushing yourself both physically and mentally. By failing to pace yourself, you will "hit the wall," like the long-distance runner who runs too fast at the beginning of the race. Overworking yourself for too long without mental and physical relaxation is a sure way to run out of steam. Learning to balance your time and set realistic expectations for yourself will prevent burnout.

7. Sometimes you put off doing something because you literally don't know how to do it. This may be hard to admit to yourself, so you may make other excuses. When you can't get started on something, consider the possibility that you need help. For example, if you get approval from your favorite instructor for a term paper topic that requires collecting data and creating graphics, you can be stymied if you don't have the necessary skills and tools to do the work and do it well. Does the collection and analysis of the data require the use of a software program that you don't have and cannot afford to buy? Sometimes it is difficult to ask for help and sometimes it is even hard to recognize that you need help. When you feel stymied, ask yourself, "Do I need help?" Do you need information but haven't a clue as to where to go to get it? Have you committed to doing something that is really beyond your level of skills? Being able to own up to personal limitations and seek out support and resources where needed is a skill used every day by highly successful people.

Moore, Rebecca, et al. "Coping with Procrastination." *College Success*. Prentice Hall, 1997.

1. What is the topic of paragraph 3?

    _____

    _____

    _____

2. What is the topic sentence of paragraph 3?

    _____

    _____

    _____

3. What is the topic of paragraph 5?

_____

_____

_____

4. In paragraph 5, the topic sentence is:

_____

_____

_____

5. What is the main idea of paragraph 4?

_____

_____

_____

6. What skills, if any, did you learn from this article that will help you avoid procrastinating?

_____

_____

_____

_____

_____

Review Your Understanding of Identifying an Essay's Thesis Statement

Longer readings, like essays, contain a topic and main idea. In essays, the main point is called the thesis statement. The thesis statement is the one idea, belief, or position the writer wants you to understand after you've finished reading. The thesis statement includes the topic and what is being said about that topic. Then, the rest of the essay works to explain, support, or drive home that thesis statement for the reader.

While thesis statements are usually in the introductory paragraph, they can be saved until the end of an essay. Typical thesis statements are one sentence, but some can be two sentences or even more. A thesis statement is going to contain two things: the topic of the essay and a claim, stance, or point about the topic. To ensure you correctly identify the thesis statement, it may be helpful to reread the essay with your selected thesis statement in mind. That way you can determine if the supporting ideas add to the identified thesis statement and if in fact you have located the thesis statement correctly. Here is an example:

I believe in a cup of coffee. Perhaps it is the sweet aroma, the feel of the coffee beans, or even just the sheer joy of the dark liquid filling your body with a pleasant warmth. I love that in the morning I can always look forward to starting off my day happily with a nice hot cup of coffee placed in my favorite beach-themed mug. I love that even if everything in my day is going wrong, the coffee is somehow the one thing that goes completely right. And although I could go on and on about my appreciation for the drink itself, what I love most is that I can invite friends and loved ones to share in a coffee experience with me.

Danielle. "A Cup of Coffee." This I Believe. 7 Jan. 2011, thisibelieve.org/essay/92485/

The thesis statement is at the end of the passage: "And although I could go on and on about my appreciation for the drink itself, what I love most is that I can invite friends and loved ones to share in a coffee experience with me." By keeping that statement in mind as you reread the passage, you can verify that it is indeed the thesis statement.

Apply Your Knowledge of Identifying an Essay's Thesis Statement

The following passage is Malala Yousafzai's Address on Education to the United Nations on July 12, 2013. She was 16 years old when she delivered this speech. Speeches are very similar to essays as they are both longer texts and have a main idea or thesis statement.

Read the passage and underline the thesis statement. Then, answer the questions that follow. Remember: while a thesis statement usually appears at the beginning of an essay, it does not have to.

Dear brothers and sisters, do remember one thing. Malala day is not my day. Today is the day of every woman, every boy and every girl who have raised their voice for their rights. There are hundreds of Human rights activists and social workers who are not only speaking for human rights, but who are struggling to achieve their goals of education, peace and equality. Thousands of people have been killed by the terrorists and millions have been injured. I am just one of them.

So here I stand.... one girl among many. I speak – not for myself, but for all girls and boys. I raise up my voice – not so that I can shout, but so that those without a voice can be heard. Those who have fought for their rights: Their right to live in peace. Their right to be treated with dignity. Their right to equality of opportunity. Their right to be educated.

Dear Friends, on the 9th of October 2012, the Taliban shot me on the left side of my forehead. They shot my friends too. They thought that the bullets would silence us. But they failed. And then, out of that silence came, thousands of voices. The terrorists thought that they would change our aims and stop our ambitions but nothing changed in my life except this: Weakness, fear and hopelessness died. Strength, power and courage was born. I am the same Malala. My ambitions are the same. My hopes are the same. My dreams are the same.

Dear sisters and brothers, I am not against anyone. Neither am I here to speak in terms of personal revenge against the Taliban or any other terrorists group. I am here to speak up for the right of education of every child. I want education for the sons and the daughters of all the extremists especially the Taliban. I do not even hate the Talib who shot me. Even if there is a gun in my hand and he stands in front of me. I would not shoot him. This is the compassion that I have learnt from Muhammad-the prophet of mercy, Jesus Christ and Lord Buddha. This is the legacy of change that I have inherited from Martin Luther King, Nelson Mandela and Muhammad Ali Jinnah. This is the philosophy of non-violence that I have learnt from Gandhi Jee, Bacha Khan and Mother Teresa. And this is the forgiveness that I have learnt from my mother and father. This is what my soul is telling me, be peaceful and love everyone.

Dear sisters and brothers, we realize the importance of light when we see darkness. We realize the importance of our voice when we are silenced. In the same way, when we were in Swat, the north of Pakistan, we realized the importance of pens and books when we saw the guns. The extremists are afraid of books and pens. The power of education frightens them. They are afraid of women. The power of the voice of women frightens them. And that is why they killed 14 innocent medical students in the recent attack in Quetta. And that is why they killed many female teachers and polio workers in Khyber Pukhtoon Khwa and FATA. That is why they are blasting schools every day. Because they were and they are afraid of change, afraid of the equality that we will bring into our society.

I remember that there was a boy in our school who was asked by a journalist, "Why are the Taliban against education?" He answered very simply. By pointing to his book he said, "A Talib doesn't know what is written inside this book." They think that God is a tiny, little conservative being who would send girls to the hell just because of going to school. The terrorists are misusing the name of Islam and Pashtun society for their own personal benefits. Pakistan is peace-loving democratic country. Pashtuns want education for their daughters and sons. And Islam is a religion of peace, humanity and brotherhood. Islam says that it is not only each child's right to get education, rather it is their duty and responsibility.

Honorable Secretary General, peace is necessary for education. In many parts of the world especially Pakistan and Afghanistan; terrorism, wars and conflicts stop children to go to their schools. We are really tired of these wars. Women and children are suffering in many parts of the world in many ways. In India, innocent and poor children are victims of child labor. Many schools have been destroyed in Nigeria. People in Afghanistan have been affected by the hurdles of extremism for decades. Young girls have to do domestic child labor and are forced to get married at early age. Poverty, ignorance, injustice, racism and the deprivation of basic rights are the main problems faced by both men and women.

Dear fellows, today I am focusing on women's rights and girls' education because they are suffering the most. There was a time when women social activists asked men to stand up for their rights. But, this time, we will do it by ourselves. I am not telling men to step away from speaking for women's rights rather I am focusing on women to be independent to fight for themselves.

Dear sisters and brothers, now it's time to speak up. So today, we call upon the world leaders to change their strategic policies in favor of peace and prosperity. We call upon the world leaders that all the peace deals must protect women and children's rights. A deal that goes against the dignity of women and their rights is unacceptable. We call upon all governments to ensure free compulsory education for every child all over the world. We call upon all governments to fight against terrorism and violence, to protect children from brutality and harm. We call upon the developed nations to support the expansion of educational opportunities for girls in the developing world. We call upon all communities to be tolerant – to reject prejudice based on cast, creed, sect, religion or gender. To ensure freedom and equality for women so that they can flourish. We cannot all succeed when half of us are held back. We call upon our sisters around the world to be brave – to embrace the strength within themselves and realize their full potential.

Dear brothers and sisters, we want schools and education for every child's bright future. We will continue our journey to our destination of peace and education for everyone. No one can stop us. We will speak for our rights and we will bring change through our voice. We must believe in the power and the strength of our words. Our words can change the world. Because we are all together, united for the cause of education. And if we want to achieve our goal, then let us empower ourselves with the weapon of knowledge and let us shield ourselves with unity and togetherness.

Dear brothers and sisters, we must not forget that millions of people are suffering from poverty, injustice and ignorance. We must not forget that millions of children are out of schools. We must not forget that our sisters and brothers are waiting for a bright peaceful future. So let us wage a global struggle against illiteracy, poverty and terrorism and let us pick up our books and pens. They are our most powerful weapons. One child, one teacher, one pen and one book can change the world. Education is the only solution. Education First.

Yousafzai, Malala. "Malala's Speech." UN.org, 2013, www.un.org/News/dh/infocus/malala_speech.pdf

1. What topic sentences and supporting details support the thesis statement that you selected for this passage?

    _____

    _____

    _____

2. How does the thesis statement in this passage differ from a thesis statement in a more traditional essay?

    _____

    _____

    _____

    _____

    _____

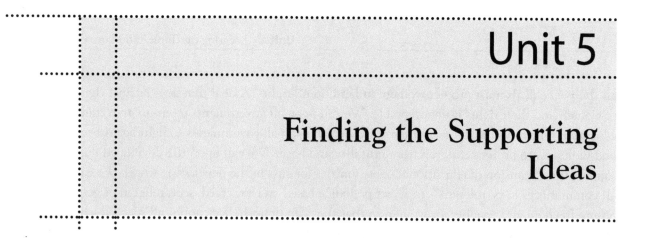

Unit 5

Finding the Supporting Ideas

Review Your Understanding of Supporting Ideas in Paragraphs and Essays

Supporting ideas explain or prove the general main idea stated in the topic sentence or thesis statement. Supporting ideas, which are found in all types of writing, from paragraph to essays to textbook readings, should answer the questions raised by the topic sentence. Supporting ideas come in the form of major details, which are the specific facts and examples that explain or support the topic sentence in a paragraph and the thesis statement in an essay. Minor details then provide more explanation and information about the major details. Here is a visual to help you think about and identify the different pieces in a reading:

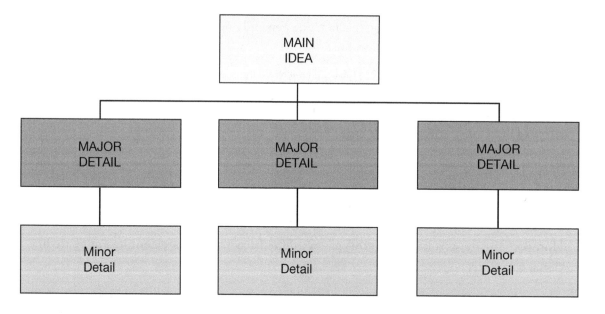

Now, let's look at the components in context, inside of a paragraph:

> Franchising arrangements fall into three general categories. In the first approach, a manufacturer authorizes a number of retail stores to sell a certain brand-name item. This franchising arrangement, one of the oldest, is prevalent in sales of passenger cars and trucks, farm equipment, shoes, paint, earth-moving equipment, and petroleum. In the second type of franchising arrangement, a producer licenses distributors to sell a given product to retailers. This arrangement is common in the soft-drink industry, where most national manufacturers of soft-drink syrups— the Coca-Cola Company, Dr Pepper/Seven-Up Companies, Pepsico, Royal Crown Companies, Inc.—franchise independent bottlers who then serve retailers. In a third form of franchising, a franchisor supplies brand names, techniques, or other services instead of a complete product. This approach to franchising, which is the most typical today, is used by Holiday Inns, the Howard Johnson Company, AAMCO Transmissions, McDonald's, Dairy Queen, Avis, the Hertz Corporation, KFC (Kentucky Fried Chicken), and SUBWAY, to name but a few.

Margin annotations: Main idea/topic sentence · Major supporting detail · Minor supporting detail · Major supporting detail · Minor supporting detail · Major supporting detail · Minor supporting detail

Pride, William M., et al. *Business*, 6th ed., Houghton Mifflin, 1999, pp. 128–29.

Although both paragraphs and essays include major and minor details, where they are in each is a bit different. The diagram below highlights the typical location of supporting ideas in paragraphs and in longer selections like essays. Each box in the diagram represents a paragraph.

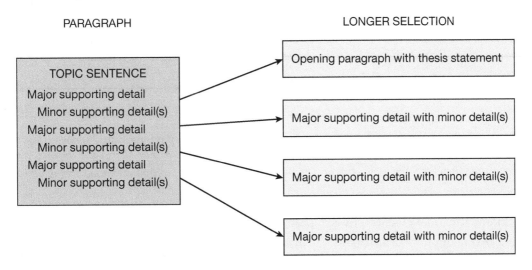

As you can see, in an essay, the supporting ideas are spread out over several paragraphs. Each of the major details is the topic of a separate paragraph, and each is developed with the examples, anecdotes, explanations, or other pieces of information that function as minor details.

Apply Your Knowledge of Supporting Ideas

Read the following topic sentences. After each topic sentence, provide a question raised by the topic sentence and a supporting idea that could answer that question.

Here is an example:

Topic Sentence: Christmas is my mom's favorite holiday.

Question: Why is Christmas her favorite holiday?

Possible supporting idea: My mom loves getting together with family, and Christmas is the perfect time to do so.

Now, it's your turn:

1. Topic Sentence: There are many reasons why air pollution has increased in the city.

    Question: _____

    Possible Idea to Answer Question: _____

    _____

2. Topic Sentence: Effective leaders share a few characteristics.

    Question: _____

    Possible Idea to Answer Question: _____

    _____

3. Topic Sentence: Cooking requires a specific set of skills.

    Question: _____

    Possible Idea to Answer Question: _____

    _____

Let's make sure you are comfortable with identifying and labeling a paragraph and essay.

Read the paragraph, and then label the topic sentence, major supporting details, and minor supporting details.

Oceanographers use the principles of physics, chemistry, mathematics, and engineering to study the oceans, including their movements, physical properties, and plant and animal life. Many oceanographers perform most of their work at sea, making observations, conducting experiments, and collecting data on tides, currents, and other phenomena. For example, they may study undersea mountain ranges, interactions of the ocean with the atmosphere, or the layers of sediment on and beneath the ocean floor. Other oceanographers work almost entirely in laboratories on land. They measure, dissect, and photograph fish; study sea specimens and plankton; identify, catalog, and analyze different kinds of sea life and minerals; and they may also be involved in plotting maps or using computers to test theories about the oceans.

Sherman, Sharon J. and Alan Sherman. *Essential Concepts of Chemistry*, 6th ed., Houghton-Mifflin, 1996, p. 270.

One final challenge in identifying supporting ideas is locating them in longer writing pieces like essays. When reading longer pieces, remember what you have learned about supporting ideas and major and minor details. Remember that major details support the thesis statement and that minor details add explanation about the major details. Sometimes it can be useful to read and annotate— marking up the text—the passage, and then go back and match the major details to the thesis statement. Do these directly support and add explanation? Then, do the same for the minor details. Do these provide more explanation and detail about the major details you identified? If not, re-read the piece and ensure you are identifying the correct parts.

Read the essay, and then label the thesis statement, major supporting details, and minor supporting details.

The Case for a Useless Degree

During my junior year of high school, I sat near the window in English class. I wanted to be an engineer, so during most classes, I daydreamed about applying early to MIT while the class rambled on about short stories by Philip Roth. But sometime in the spring, not long after we'd finished a lesson about some strange thing called "transcendentalism," and started reading Shakespeare, I kicked my best friend Crary's chair.

Henry David Thoreau and Elizabethan sonnets had suddenly piqued[1] my interest—I was fascinated, bewildered, hooked. Since his mother had been forcing books on him since he was 3 months old, Crary seemed to know everything about everything. "Where does any of this lead?" I asked him. "There's a major in college called comparative literature," he said. "They read books together like this all day long." It sounded intriguing, but I was dumbfounded. "What in the world would be the value in that?"

I later learned that there's actually a huge value in it. Computer science, accounting, marketing—the purpose of many majors is self-evident. They lead to well-paid jobs and clear-cut career paths. (One hopes, at least.) But comparative literature, classics, and philosophy—according to the new conventional wisdom—offer no clear trajectory. As my colleague Nancy Cook reports, many schools are even slashing liberal arts from their curriculum. It's true that studying the humanities will surely elicit snide comments from your uncle like, "All that studying so you'll be able to ask, 'You want fries with that?'" Tell your uncle to shove it. Majoring in the liberal arts is still the best use of your college tuition.

A degree in history or religion or languages can be anything you want it to be. Say you're interested in a career that makes lots of money. After a few years of work, an M.B.A. would be a good bet. But an undergraduate degree in business isn't necessarily going to give you a leg up. "We obviously take people with marketing or business backgrounds," says Bruce DelMonico, director of admissions at the Yale School of Management, "But we don't value those over liberal arts or humanities backgrounds." Stats don't lie. One in five of the school's 2010 class was a business major, the same number majored in humanities. "It's not a question of, 'do you have the particular classes,' but it's do you have the mind-set, the temperament, the intellectual horsepower to succeed?"

In your first job out of college, pretty much everything is going to be learned at work. From there, erecting a successful career means moving onto a new position by building on prior work experience more than it does falling back on a Methods of Accounting or Communicating Your Message Effectively class from your junior year. In fact, there is a good chance that when you're pitted up against four other candidates and you can explain to the hiring manager how your history degree has helped you understand complex problems in perspective, you'll stand apart as someone who's more insightful than the others who are just toeing the line.

For centuries, Ivy League institutions have considered the liberal arts the bedrock of a sound education. In 1919, Columbia College began offering its Contemporary Civilization class, a cornerstone of its "core curriculum," which the school still demands of every undergraduate today. "The Core classroom thrives on the most difficult questions in the human experience," the school's Web site explains. Through classes in the humanities, writing, foreign languages and sciences, Columbia develops in its undergraduates, "critical tools of observation, evaluation, and judgment that translate into all spheres of life." Evidenced by its estimable reputation—as well as its long list of wildly successful alumni—the plan demonstrates the value of a well-rounded undergraduate experience. But you don't have to go to Columbia, Harvard, or Yale to get it—I studied philosophy and, yes, comparative literature at the State University of New York at Binghamton. And, 10 years hence, I've found that these kinds of "critical tools" reap endless benefits.

Of course, my case crumbles if you want to, say, go to medical school. Or be an engineer. Or be a nurse. In that case, you're pretty much bound to studying chemistry, physics, or biology. It would be absurd to suggest that studying poststructuralist French literary theory (which is what I did, and the wisdom of that exact decision is for another discussion) would make you a great neurosurgeon. It wouldn't. But the vast majority of professional fields—from the law, to the military, to writing, to academics, to teaching, to hospitality, to administration, to management, to business, the list goes on and on—can be had with a strong, foundational, liberal-arts degree.

When being tried for his life, Socrates offered up a defense of philosophy by declaring that, "the unexamined life is not worth living." Who would disagree with that? But more importantly, being able to engage others intelligently about art, music, and politics may actually make you an enjoyable person to be around. I'm not suggesting that all computer science or physics majors are bores. I mean, Google founder Sergey Brin is unquestionably on my top-five-people-to-have-dinner-with list. But even in this relentlessly digital age, there's much to be said about learning about what it means to be human. And yes, that can indeed get you a good job. As for my friend Crary? He studied history. And now he's climbing the ranks at one of the country's premier law firms.

Blast, Andrew. "The Case for a Useless Degree." *Newsweek*, 2010.

Unit 6

Understanding Implied Ideas and Inferences

Review Your Understanding of Determining the Implied Main Ideas

Every piece of writing contains a main idea. Sometimes that main idea is stated outright in a topic sentence or a thesis statement. Sometime, though, the main is implied. An implied main idea is one that is suggested but not said. It is a little trickier to identify an implied main idea rather than one that is stated, but it is possible. The best way to figure out an implied main ides is to first locate the supporting ideas of the paragraph or essay. These will provide hints, clues, and information that you can use to start to decipher the main idea. Then, considering all of those details together, you can make a generalization about the ideas discussed in the supporting ideas to help you make a conclusion about what the text is really about or what the writer is trying to say. Here are the three steps in order:

To determine the implied main idea, there is a 3-step process you should follow:

1. Find the topic of each sentence.

2. Determine a general topic based on the details provided (hint: you can make a generalization about your list of sentence or paragraph topics).

3. State the implied main idea.

As an example, let's go through all three steps for this paragraph:

(1) Emory University historian Michael Bellesiles, author of the critically acclaimed but controversial book *Arming America: The Origins of a National Gun Culture*, said some of his crucial research notes had been destroyed in a flood in his office. (2) He said he had relied on microfilm records in the federal archive in East Point, Georgia, but it has no such records. (3) He said he had examined probate records in 30 places around the country, such as the San Francisco Superior Court, but those records were destroyed in the 1906 earthquake. (4) Well, then, he said he had seen them in the Contra Costa County Historical Society, but the society has no such records, and no record of Bellesiles's visiting the society. (5) Then he said he did the research somewhere else but is not sure where. (6) Researchers have found that he consistently misrepresents extant records in Providence, Rhode Island, and Vermont. (7) When he tried to buttress his case by posting evidence on his website, critics found grave errors there, too, and he blamed the errors on a hacker breaking into his files.

Will, George F. "Gunning for a Bad Book." *Newsweek*, 30 May 2002.

Step 1:   Sentence 1: Bellesiles's explanation of his research notes

Sentence 2: No such records exist

Sentence 3: Records were destroyed

Sentence 4: No record of visit

Sentence 5: Not sure where research was done

Sentence 6: Misrepresents existing records

Sentence 7: Errors on website, blames hackers

Step 2:   Paragraph's Topic: Bellesiles's questionable research

Step 3:   Implied Main Idea: The many excuses and untruths Bellesiles offers about his research indicate that his book is not based on reliable facts.

Apply Your Understanding of Implied Main Ideas

The following paragraphs do not include a stated main idea. After reading the paragraphs, follow the 3-step process detailed above. Find the topic of each sentence. Once you have those written down, make a generalization about them to help you understand the general topic. Then, determine the implied main idea for each paragraph.

Passage 1

(1) Judge Larry Standley of Harris County, Texas, required a man who slapped his wife to sign up for a yoga class as part of his punishment. (2) Municipal Judge Frances Gallegos in Santa Fe often sentences people convicted of domestic violence or fighting to a twice-a-week, New Age anger-management class, where offenders experience tai chi, meditation, acupuncture, and Eastern philosophy as means of controlling rage. (3) Municipal Judge David Hostetler of Coshocton, Ohio, ordered a man who had run away from police after a traffic accident to jog for an hour every other day around the block where the jail is located. (4) Hostetler also received worldwide attention in 2001 when he ordered two men to dress in women's clothing and walk down Main Street as a sentence for throwing beer bottles at a car and taunting a woman. (5) Judge Mike Erwin of Baton Rouge ordered a young man who hit an elderly man in an argument to listen to a John Prine song, "Hello in There," about lonely senior citizens and write an essay about it.

Leinwand, Donna. "Judges Write Creative Sentences." *USA Today*, 24 Feb. 2004, p. 3A.

Topic of Sentence 1: _____

Topic of Sentence 2: _____

Topic of Sentence 3: _____

Topic of Sentence 4: _____

Topic of Sentence 5: _____

Generalized Topic: _____

Implied Main Idea: _____

Passage 2

(1) When people don't listen well on the job, they may miss information that can affect their professional effectiveness and advancement. (2) In a survey, 1,000 human resource professionals ranked listening as the number one quality of effective managers. (3) Skill in listening is also linked to resolving workplace conflicts. (4) Doctors who don't listen fully to patients may misdiagnose or mistreat medical problems. (5) Ineffective listening in the classroom diminishes learning and performance on tests. (6) In personal relationships, poor listening can hinder understanding of others, and listening ineffectively to public communication leaves us uninformed about civic issues.

Wood, Julia T. "Chapter 4." *Communication in Our Lives*, 6th ed, Wadsworth, 2012, pp. 74–75.

Topic of Sentence 1: _____

Topic of Sentence 2: _____

Topic of Sentence 3: _____

Topic of Sentence 4: _____

Topic of Sentence 5: _____

Generalized Topic: _____

Implied Main Idea: _____

Passage 3

(1) Tornadoes have accomplished some astonishing feats, such as lifting a railroad coach with its 117 passengers and dumping it in a ditch 80 feet away. (2) Showers of toads and frogs have poured out of a cloud after tornadic winds sucked them up from a nearby pond. (3) Other oddities include chickens losing all of their feathers, pieces of straw being driven into metal pipes, and frozen hot dogs being driven into concrete walls. (4) Miraculous events have occurred, too. (5) In one instance, a schoolhouse was demolished and the 85 students inside were carried over 100 yards without one of them being killed.

Ahrens, C. Donald and Perry Samson. "Chapter 12." *Extreme Weather and Climate*, 1st ed., Brooks/Cole, 2011, p. 339.

Topic of Sentence 1: _____

Topic of Sentence 2: _____

Topic of Sentence 3: _____

Topic of Sentence 4: _____

Topic of Sentence 5: _____

Generalized Topic: _____

Implied Main Idea: _____

Review Your Understanding of Inferences

An inference is a conclusion that based upon state information, implied information, and your own knowledge of the Topic. You already make inferences all the time. And, in fact, you made inferences when you were determining the implied main ideas of the passages above. Any time you consider a group of related ideas and draw conclusions about the point they suggest, you are inferring. But you can make many mother kinds of smaller inferences as well. These inferences can be about people, situations, what you watch, and what you read.

Applying Your Understanding of Inferences

In this paragraph, you must notice details in order to make the right inferences. First, read the passage. While you read, underline supporting ideas that you can use to make inferences about the passage. Once you have completed that, answer the questions that follow.

In the United States, a great deal of effort is put into to mystifying and hiding social class differences. Students and adults alike routinely wear clothes and buy cars, homes, and other material possessions that are more expensive than they can afford in order to be perceived as being wealthier than they are. The media takes part in these deceptions by presenting the illusion that the United States is an egalitarian society in which everyone has an equal chance to succeed and attempts to either downplay the existence of the poor by failing to feature images and perspectives that present the needs and issues of the poor or by portraying the poor as undeserving and as having only themselves to blame for their position in life. When it comes to SES (socioeconomic status), myths abound. For example, many believe that the United States is mostly a middle-class country, with the wealth distributed mainly within the middle class. Contrary to this belief, U.S. Census Bureau reports reveal that less than 20 percent of the population in the United States own more than 80 percent of the wealth. That means 80 percent of the wealth may never change hands; leaving only 20 percent of the total wealth in the United States for all other individuals to work to attain.

Spradlin, Lynn. *Diversity Matters*, 2nd ed., Cengage Learning, 2012.

Now that you have Underlined the supporting ideas, what inferences can you make about this passage?

Inference 1: _____

Inference 2: _____

Read the following passages. For each passage, put a checkmark beside all of the accurate inferences provided in the list.

Passage 1

Any dog can sleep all day. The profoundness of my dog's laziness comes not from his immobility but from his almost predatory pursuit of ease. Example: He long ago learned that he can avoid the inconvenience of walking down the hall for a drink of water before bedtime by standing beside my own bedside cup of water and making a discontented, growly noise that sounds and functions exactly like a fussy old man clearing his throat. I am supposed to hold the cup under his nose for him so he can lap up all the water, then get out of bed to refill it. When I return, he will be sitting on my pillow, having taken my warm place on the bed. This happens every night. It used to be cute.

Dudley, David. "The Laziest Dog in the World." *Modern Maturity*, Jan./Feb. 2002, p. 54.

1.   The dog sleeps in the bed with the narrator. _____

2.   The narrator loves the dog. _____

3.   The narrator works as a dog trainer. _____

4.   The dog is a puppy. _____

5.   The dog is disabled. _____

Now, choose one of the inferences above and state how you know that inference is correct. What information from the passage led you to that inference?

_____

_____

_____

_____

Passage 2

If there are 1,000 square feet in the two-bedroom flat, then a good 80 percent of that space is devoted to Jim Breidenbach's passion. Yes, there are those commemorative programs that vendors hawk at most sporting events. But much of Breidenbach's collection consists of one-of-a-kind items, like a poster from the 1971 Muhammad Ali/Joe Frazier fight at Madison Square Garden. He has part of a seat from the old Madison Square Garden in one bedroom. He also has the ticket stub from the last hockey game played at the old Garden at 50th Street and Eighth Avenue—right next to a ticket stub from the first hockey game played at the new one. And somebody could just about outfit a whole hockey team in sticks, jerseys, and pucks in Breidenbach's apartment.

Richardson, Clem. "Stuck on Pucks." *New York Daily News*, 22 Mar. 2004, p. 15.

1. Jim Breidenbach is a fanatical sports fan. _____

2. Jim Breidenbach lives in Brooklyn, New York. _____

3. Jim Breidenbach is not married. _____

4. Jim Breidenbach has an impressive collection of sports memorabilia. _____

5. Jim Breidenbach enjoys hockey. _____

Now, choose one of the inferences above and state how you know that inference is correct. What information from the passage led you to that inference?

_____

_____

_____

_____

Passage 3

Every surface in my bathroom is covered with bottles of face moisturizer, body lotion, volumizer, night cream, and eye serum. On the shelves in my shower, I have 9 shampoos, 5 conditioners, and 10 bath gels. When I leave every morning, I cart 6 mascaras and 12 lip glosses in my makeup bag, just for the day, just for the office. I find myself wandering into beauty boutiques and drugstores every day scanning whether I'd truly tried each beauty potion available in the store.

Wells, Linda. "The High Road, and the Low." *Allure*, Oct. 2001, p. 70.

1. The author shops a lot. _____

2. The author is allergic to many cosmetics. _____

3. The author cares about her appearance. _____

4. The author enjoys using body lotion, shampoo, bath gels, and other beauty products. _____

5. The author is in her 20s. _____

Now, choose one of the inferences above and state how you know that inference is correct. What information from the passage led you to that inference?

_____

_____

_____

_____

Unit 7

Reading and Viewing Critically

Review Your Understanding of Distinguishing Fact from Opinion

Telling the difference between fact and opinion matters because you will see both as supporting details in material that you read. To determine the credibility of a reading, author, or website, you will have to figure out what is true, and therefore a fact, and what the author believes, which is opinion.

Facts include information that can be verified, confirmed, or proven. They will include direct experience, observation, or specific data (numbers, dates, times, or other specifics), and they also include names of people, places, and events.

Here is an example of a fact:

In 2017, 8.6 million people resided in New York City, New York.

We know this is a fact because it can be verified, it includes a year (2017), and has a number or data (8.6 million).

Opinions express beliefs, feelings, judgements, attitudes, and preferences. They cannot be verified because they are based on an individual's perceptions. People can argue about opinions and often do. Opinions include clue words that indicate the relative nature (i.e. bigger, most important, silliest) or are made up of biased language.

Here is an example of an opinion (with bias):

Driving in New York City is the worst; it is so hectic and stressful.

We know this is an opinion because it includes the subjective terms "worst," "hectic," and "stressful," which show bias. With the use of "worst," we have to ask ourselves two questions: 1) the "worst" what?, and 2) compared to driving in what other places or cities? "Hectic" and "stressful" show bias since another person may not be phased at all by driving in New York City; he or she may even consider it fun or invigorating.

Apply Your Understanding of Distinguishing Fact from Opinion

Read the passages and then label each of the sentences in the list "F" if it offers a fact and "O" if it offers an opinion.

Passage 1

(1) To me, presenting an engagement ring is the height of romantic gestures, and I don't believe women should play much of a role in its purchase. (2) Other than announcing a preference on metal or a stone's cut, they shouldn't dictate its precise design. (3) And they certainly should not mandate its expected value. (4) An engagement ring represents a guy's commitment to the woman in his life, not his commitment to make her ring finger stand apart amid her friends and family. (5) The value of the ring is in its sentiment, represented by the effort a man puts into its selection, not the dollars he puts into its acquisition.

Opdyke, Jeff D. "Bridging the Engagement-Ring Divide." *The Sun News*, 30 May 2004, p. 11D.

Sentence 1 _____

Sentence 2 _____

Sentence 3 _____

Sentence 4 _____

Sentence 5 _____

Passage 2

(1) *E Pluribus Unum* means "out of many, one." (2) No other country on earth is as multiracial and multicultural as the United States of America. (3) This diversity is a popular topic and common buzzword in newspaper and magazine articles focusing on the future of American organizations. (4) The strength of many other nations lies in their homogeneity.[1] (5) Japan is mostly made up of persons of Japanese descent, and their economy and business transactions reflect this heritage. (6) The People's Republic of China is populated mostly with persons of Chinese ancestry, whose values and culture are a major part of their global economic strength. (7) But America has always been the "melting pot" of all the world's cultures. (8) This diversity now represents the country's biggest crisis as well as its greatest opportunity.

Reece, Barry L. and Rhonda Brandt. *Effective Human Relations in Organizations*, 7th ed., Houghton Mifflin, 1999, pp. 388–89.

Sentence 1 _____

Sentence 2 _____

Sentence 3 _____

Sentence 4 _____

Sentence 5 _____

Sentence 6 _____

_____

1. homogeneity: state of being similar

Sentence 7 _____

Sentence 8 _____

Review Your Understanding of Recognizing Bias

Biased language is all around us. It includes words or expressions that may seem prejudiced, hurtful, narrow-minded, or offensive. For example, biased language may exclude or negatively reference people due to age, gender, race, ethnicity, social class, or mental or physical traits.

When bias is present in language, the language will seem imbalanced or lacking a fair representation of a topic or subject. Authors may include bias in their writing. Sometimes this is unconscious or not intended; other times, the author uses bias in an attempt to sway your opinion of the topic, encouraging you to see their side or agree with them.

Here is an example of a sentence without bias:

She has been emotional since elementary school.
Here is a similar example that includes bias:
She has been a cry-baby since she was very young.

Bias is present in the term "cry-baby," which is more negative than "emotional." Also, the author's opinion of "very young" may be different from "since elementary school" or the reader's interpretation.

Apply Your Understanding of Recognizing Bias

In each of the following statements, underline the words or phrases that reveal the author's bias. Then, on the blank, write "P" if the words encourage you to feel positive about the subject or "N" if they urge you to feel negative.

Passage 1

This summer, TV is giving us too much of a bad thing. With Fox and NBC in the forefront, the networks have offered viewers an unusually full schedule of flat sitcoms, dull dramas, and cheap, mean-spirited, copycat reality shows. Viewer response has been a resounding "no thanks."

Biano, Robert. "Networks Are Sweating Out Their Own Long, Hot Summer." *USA Today*, 30 June 2004, p. 3D.

_____

Passage 2

That the world has changed in meaningful ways since 1954 is beyond question. Oprah Winfrey and her activities were driving forces in many of those changes. Her enormously influential talk show, her philanthropic work with children in Africa and elsewhere, her popular book club and magazine, her empowering spiritual message, her contribution (by action and example) to improving race relations—all speak to the human family, touching hearts and leaving each one uplifted.

Poiter, Sidney. "Heroes and Icons: Oprah Winfrey." *Time*, 26 Apr. 2004, p. 123.

Passage 3

When we think of felines, we think of selfish, indulgent, petulant independence. It's a personality that makes us slightly uneasy: Although we believe we have a certain level of control—after all, we do feed and house this beast—we also know that the cat is quite capable of acting against immediate best interests by biting the finger of the hand that feeds it. You can't relax around a cat, which is why cats may be this era's pet. We can't relax anymore, period. Cats mock our pretensions to power, show no gratitude, and hide when we want to display them to company. They are tiny terrorists, reminders of our vulnerability.

Lipsyte, Robert. "Uncertain Times Turn Us into Cat People." *USA Today*, 30 June 2004, p. 13A.

Passage 4

At the broadest level, education is the institution within the social structure that is responsible for the formal transmission of knowledge. It is one of our most enduring and familiar institutions. Nearly 3 of every 10 people in the United States participate in education on a daily basis as either students or staff. As former students, parents, or taxpayers, all of us are involved in education in one way or another. The obvious purpose of schools is to transmit knowledge and skills. In schools, we learn how to read, write, and do arithmetic. We also learn the causes of the American War of Independence and the parts of a cell. In this way, schools ensure that each succeeding generation will have the skills needed to keep society running smoothly.

Brinkerhoff, David B., et al. "Chapter 12." *Essentials of Sociology*, 8th ed, Wadsworth, 2011, p. 284.

Review Your Understanding of Figurative Language

Authors choose to use figurative language when they want to stray away from the literal meaning of words or phrases. Their choices allow for their writing to become more effective, persuasive, or impactful. Figurative language also allows readers to relate more easily with what they read; such language can even apply to the reader's senses.

Here is a quick review of the figurative language covered in this Unit:

Simile	A comparison between two things, using "like" or "as." Example: Her eyes sparkle like diamonds.
Metaphor	A comparison where one thing is presented as what it is being compared to. Example: Her eyes were diamonds.

Hyperbole	An extreme exaggeration, could be impossible. Example: Her eyes never blinked.
Idiom	A common, everyday phrase that has a deeper meaning. Example: She and I don't see eye to eye.
Imagery	When figurative language is used to represent or portray objects, actions, or ideas so they appeal to the reader's senses. Example: Her eyes were such a bright green, they almost glowed.

Apply Your Understanding of Figurative Language

Read each example and determine which figurative language technique is being used: simile, metaphor, hyperbole, imagery, or idiom. Then, provide an explanation of how or why you determined your answer.

1. Like burnt-out torches by a sick man's bed

    What technique is this? _____

    Explanation: _____

    _____

    _____

    _____

    _____

2. The moon was a ghostly galleon tossed upon cloudy seas, / The road was a ribbon of moon-light over the purple moor

    What technique is this? _____

    Explanation: _____

    _____

    _____

    _____

    _____

3. Your speech evokes a thousand sympathies

    What technique is this? _____

    Explanation: _____

    _____

    _____

    _____

    _____

4. Break a leg!

What technique is this? _____

Explanation: _____

_____

_____

_____

_____

5. Glittering white, the blanket of snow covered everything in sight.

What technique is this? _____

Explanation: _____

_____

_____

_____

_____

Review Your Understanding of Interpreting Data and Information: Maps, Charts, and Graphs

Today, you would have to search far and wide to find a single informational text without one or more graphical or visual elements. Such elements, including maps, charts, and graphs, are included to appeal to a wide range of audiences and to increase the text's diversity, complexity, and importance. Also, sometimes a visual is the best way to present information and data. If you do not know how to decode and interpret visual aids, you will be at a large disadvantage when trying to understand, analyze, and respond to texts that include them. A large part of being able to decipher visual aids is knowing why they are used, the types of data they display, and the kinds of questions they can answer. Here is an overview of the visual aids covered in this unit:

Type of Visual Aid	What Used For
Maps	Included as a visual representation of an area and its physical characteristics. Can be used to show borders, distances, or to compare. Question a Map Could Answer: How far is this country from this country?
Organizational Chart	Used to represent the lines of authority and responsibility within an organization. Has branching lines that descend from each box to represent the sequence or steps. Question an Organizational Chart Could Answer: Who reports directly to the CEO of Amazon?

Flow Chart	Represents the sequence of steps or stages within a workflow or process; usually connected with lines and arrows. Question a Flow Chart Could Answer: What is the third step in this process?
Pie Chart	Displays data as percentages or proportions; usually color-coded. Easy way to compare 6 categories or fewer. Question a Pie Chart Could Answer: What percentage of women are married?
Line Graph	Reveals changes or trends in numerical data over time; show how 2 factors interact with one another. Question a Line Graph Could Answer: In 2010, how many people paid for cable?
Bar Graph	Indicate quantities of something with bars or rectangles at different heights; each bar is labeled to show what is being measured. May not include a time factor but focuses on quantities instead. Question a Bar Graph Could Answer: After surveying 150 people, how many of them prefer romance movies over the other choices?

Apply Your Understanding of Interpreting Data and Information: Maps, Charts, and Graphs

Study the visual aids provided, and then answer the questions that follow.

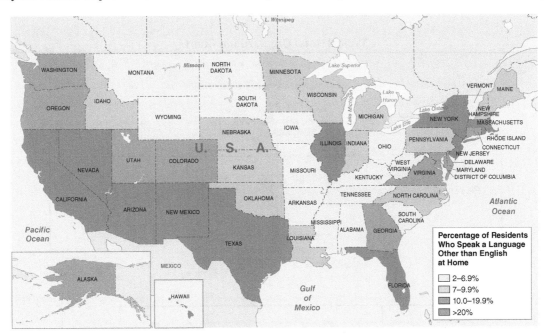

1. What does this visual represent? _____

_____

2. Name three states in which 20 percent or more of the residents speak a language other than English at home. _____

_____

_____

3. Name three states in which only 2 to 6.9 percent of the residents speak a language other than English at home. _____

_____

_____

4. What percent of residents in Colorado speak a language other than English at home?
_____

_____

5. What percent of residents in Indiana speak a language other than English at home?

_____

6. What is the source of this visual? _____

_____

_____

Typical Hotel Organization Chart

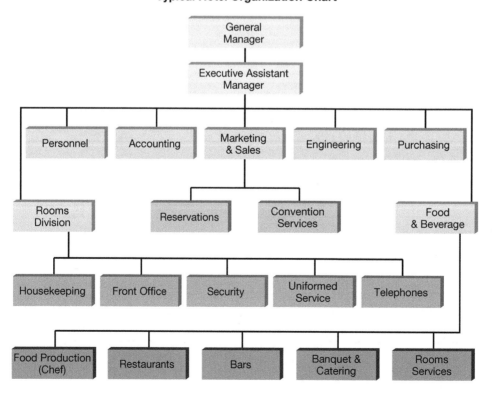

1. What is the title of the person with the most responsibility in this organization?

    _____

    _____

2. Who reports directly to the General Manager? _____

    _____

    _____

3. How many departments report directly to the Executive Assistant Manager? _____

    List two of these departments. _____

    _____

    _____

4. List the two groups that report directly to Marketing and Sales Department. _____

    _____

    _____

5. What department does housekeeping report to? _____

    _____

6. Which groups (there are 5) report to the Food and Beverage Department? _____

    _____

    _____

    _____

Unit 8

Recognizing Patterns of Organization

Review Your Understanding of Transitions and Patterns of Organization

Transitions are words or phrases used to show the relationships between thoughts and ideas. These thoughts and ideas can be in supporting details, sentences, or paragraphs. Transitions make sentences clearer, so they help readers understand the ideas in a passage more easily. Without them, you would have to figure out the relationships on your own.

As a reminder, transitions have three characteristics (these will help you pick them out later):

1. They may be synonyms for each other. They may mean the same thing or be used interchangeably. This is especially true in a paragraph or essay where multiple transitions need to be used for one pattern of organization. If you list more than one example, you will need more than one transition.

   a. For example: "In addition" is the same as "Also" and "Too"

2. Some can be used to show more than one kind of relationship between details. This means, the same transition may appear in more than one pattern of organization.

   a. The *next* component of love is commitment. (list of items)

   b. *Next*, prepare an agenda for the meeting. (steps in a process)

3. Different transitions can create a small but an important change for the meaning of a sentence or paragraph. Let's look at an example you have already seen from Unit 8.

   a. She was afraid of guns. *But* she bought a gun and learned to use it to protect herself. (says: she did so even though she did not want to and was scared)

   b. She was afraid of guns. *So* she bought a gun and learned how to use it to protect herself. (says: she did so in order to get over hear fear)

Identifying and understanding the purpose of transitions is important, especially when you are trying to figure out the pattern of organization used in a reading. That is because certain transitions can hint at the pattern being used by the author. Likewise, the pattern used will call for certain transitions in order for the sentences, paragraphs, and relationships to make sense. So transitions play an important role in evaluating a reading.

48

The specific pattern of organization (or combination of patterns) used in a reading depends on the topic and the author's objectives or purpose. Unit 8 introduced you to six of the most common patterns of organizations; here is a quick review of those patterns:

Pattern of Organization	Why Use It?
Definition	A pattern of writing that states the meaning of a particular word, term, or concept, and then goes on to illustrate it with one or more examples.
Time Order (chronological, process)	A pattern of writing where details are arranged according to their chronological relationships or in the order in which they happened or should happen.
Cause/Effect	A pattern of writing that presents a series of occurrences by showing how one led to another.
Compare/Contrast	A pattern of writing that explains the similarities and/or the differences between two or more things.
Example	A pattern of writing that illustrates a core topic by providing at least one example.
Classification	A pattern of writing that explains a core topic by dividing it into smaller parts or by grouping its related items or events.

While some paragraphs and essays only use one pattern, most of them incorporate at least two.

Now let's look at the common transitions used in each pattern:

Pattern of Organization	Common Transitions
Definition	The definition of, is defined as, the meaning of, to describe, to translate
Time Order (chronological, process)	First, second, third, next, finally, before, when, over time, in the beginning, meanwhile, eventually
Cause/Effect	Led to, resulted in, chain reaction, because, so, factors, affect
Compare/Contrast	Similarly, in contrast, different, alike, just as, unlike, however, as opposed to, in reality, but, yet
Example	For example, for instance, first of all, most importantly, in addition, another, finally, lastly, furthermore
Classification	Classified as, divided into, type, parts, separated into, component of, categorized, is related to/associated with

Apply Your Understanding of Transitions and Patterns of Organization

Read each of the following paragraphs and underline the transition words or phrases. Then, in the list below the paragraph, place a check mark next to the patterns used to organize the details—keep in mind that more than one pattern may be used. Also, remember that you can determine the organizational patterns by the transitions you find.

1. Although Columbus was a great navigator and sailor, he was not a particularly good leader. Spanish officials and settlers were never loyal to him, and King Ferdinand and Queen Isabella of Spain eventually tired of him. However, unlike Columbus, Hernando Cortés was a great leader and was able to help Ferdinand and Isabella realize their goals. In 1519, he and an army of six hundred Spanish soldiers landed in Mexico. Within three years, Cortés and his small force had defeated the mighty Aztec empire. Establishing themselves in Mexico City, the Spanish took over the empire, bringing the Indian groups to the south under their rule.

   Adapted from Berkin, Carol, et al. *Making America*, Brief 2nd ed., Houghton Mifflin Co., 2001, p. 26.

   Time order _____

   Cause/effect _____

   Comparison/contrast _____

   Definition _____

2. If you feel like giving up when you encounter a very long or hard assignment, you probably have a low tolerance for unpleasant tasks. However, you can change your attitude toward unpleasant tasks so that you can concentrate and get them done. First, remind yourself that the sooner you start, the sooner you will finish. Next, remind yourself that your attitude toward studying may be causing you to lose concentration and may be keeping you from doing your work as well as you can. Third, make long or difficult assignments easier to handle by breaking them into smaller segments that you can complete in one sitting. Then reward yourself for doing the work.

   Adapted from Kanar, Carol C. *The Confident Student*, 5th ed., Houghton Mifflin Co., 2004, p. 258.

   Process _____

   Cause/effect _____

   Comparison/contrast _____

   Example _____

3. Readers fall into two categories: active readers and passive readers. *Active readers* control their interest level and concentration. They read with a purpose. They know what information to look for and why. Active readers constantly question what they read. They relate the author's ideas to their own experience and prior knowledge. On the other hand, *passive readers* are not in control of their reading. They read the same way they watch television programs and movies, expecting others to engage them and keep their attention. A common passive reading experience is to "wake up" in the middle of a paragraph, wondering what you have just read. Active readers control the process of reading; passive readers are unaware that reading *is* a process that they can control.

   Kanar, Carol. *The Confident Student*, 7th ed., Wadsworth, 2011, p. 162.

Classification _____

Process _____

Cause/effect _____

Comparison/contrast _____

4. Because so many children play at the Lexington Avenue Park every day, many children lose the toys they bring to play with, such as trucks, dolls, and balls. You can do a few things to avoid losing your children's toys at the park. Before you come to the park, label everything with your child's name and address. It is also a good idea to bring as few toys as you can and to make a list of the things that you bring with you. While you are at the park, keep your child's toys in a pile where he or she is playing, if possible. Before you leave, make a quick sweep of the park to see if your child has left anything behind. This will ensure that you leave with your child's toys.

Time order _____

Cause/effect _____

Comparison/contrast _____

Definition _____

The following groups of sentences have been scrambled. Number them in the order they should appear (1, 2, 3, and so on) so that they make sense. Use the transitions to help you figure out the right order. Then, determine the pattern(s) used by placing a check mark next to the pattern or patterns used to organize the details.

1. _____ First, write your positive statements—sentences like "I am intelligent," "I can handle my problems," and "I am creative"—on 3 3 5 index cards.

   _____ One technique for improving self-esteem is designing positive self-talk statements.

   _____ Then, each time you see one of these cards, review its message and believe the words.

   _____ Next, attach your cards to your bathroom mirror, your refrigerator, your car dashboard, and your desk.

Adapted from Reece, Barry L. and Rhonda Brandt. *Effective Human Relations in Organizations*, 7th ed., Houghton Mifflin Co., 1997, p. 111.

Pattern of organization:

Time order _____

Cause/effect _____

Comparison/contrast _____

Process _____

2. _____ The catalog will also tell you whether a fee is involved in applying for a degree and under what conditions you can get your money back if you withdraw from a course.

_____ The calendar in your catalog, for example, is one of the items you will use most frequently.

_____ Your college catalog is a publication that contains a wealth of information about your college's programs, policies, requirements, and services.

_____ It shows when classes begin and end, when holidays occur, when the drop-and-add period is over, when final exams are scheduled, and when you should apply for a degree.

Adapted from Kanar, Carol C. *The Confident Student*, 5th ed., Houghton Mifflin Co., 2004, p. 20.

Pattern of organization:

Chronological _____

Cause/effect _____

Comparison/contrast _____

Definition _____

3. _____ Consequently, town residents who want to swim will have to join either the Silver Lake swim club or the Charles Cook Pool in Cortlandt Manor.

_____ As a result, no swimming will be allowed during July and August.

_____ Due to high levels of algae, the Duck Pond in the center of town has tested positive for a dangerous microbe.

_____ Because swimming won't be allowed, the Duck Pond in the center of town is being closed for the summer.

Pattern of organization:

Time order _____

Cause/effect _____

Comparison/contrast _____

Example _____

4. _____ In the early 1960s, Irving refined his storytelling skills at the University of Iowa, where he got a master's degree in creative writing.

_____ John Irving grew up in Exeter, New Hampshire, where his stepfather taught at the exclusive Phillips Exeter Academy.

_____ He took up wrestling at age fourteen to provide a much-needed outlet for his energy.

_____ In 1964, he married photographer Shyla Leary, whom he met in college, and became a father at the age of 23.

Adapted from Hubbard, Kim Hubbard and Natasha Stoynoff. "Hands Full." *Magazine*, 30 July 2001, pp. 96–97.

Pattern of organization:

Chronological _____

Cause/effect _____

Comparison/contrast_____

Example_____

Read the following passages and answer the questions that follow.

History of Theme Parks

The historical roots of theme parks originate in the fair. Historians note that fairs have existed for thousands of years, and the earliest fairs were probably agricultural shows. Today the agricultural fair is still the most common type held in the United States and Canada. Fairs also usually offer musical entertainment, sports events, and carnival rides and games. In addition to agricultural fairs, international expositions like the World's Fair highlight scientific, industrial, and artistic contributions from various countries.

From the temporary, seasonal operation of the local fair sprang the idea for the development of permanent amusement parks. One of the earliest known amusement parks was Vauxhall Gardens in England, created in the 1600s. Copenhagen's Tivoli Gardens, which celebrated its 150th anniversary in August 1993, is probably the world's most famous amusement park. Tivoli contains twenty acres of gardens, twenty-five rides, and more than twenty-five restaurants. One roller-coaster ride, called the Flying Trunk, takes travelers through a fairy-tale world of Hans Christian Andersen characters. The Tivoli Gardens, visited by Walt Disney, provided some of the inspiration for his Disneyland development.

Amusement parks were first built in the United States in the 1800s at popular beaches. The major attraction was often a roller coaster, originally called a "sliding hill." The establishment of Coney Island in 1895, however, took amusement parks to a new level. Located in Brooklyn, New York, on the Atlantic Ocean, Coney Island was (and still is) a popular tourist attraction known for its amusement facilities, boardwalk, beaches, and the New York Aquarium.

Such amusement parks were, of course, the predecessors to modern-day theme parks. Today's theme parks have exploited the thrills of amusement park rides and combined them with the educational entertainment of fairs. A theme park differs from an amusement park in two distinct ways. First, theme parks are based on a particular setting or artistic interpretation such as "Frontierland" or "Old Country." Second, theme parks usually operate on a much larger scale than amusement parks, with hundreds or thousands of acres of parkland and hundreds or thousands of employees running the operation.

The primary purpose of a theme park was best described by the father of theme parks, Walt Disney. He thought that theme parks should be clean, friendly places where people could have a good time. In July 1955, Disney opened the world's first theme park, Disneyland, in Anaheim, California. The face of family recreation has never been the same. Legend has it that Walt Disney conceived his theme park idea while sitting on a park bench watching his daughters ride a merry-go-round. He thought that adults should have the chance to enjoy themselves, too, rather than just pay the tab. Accordingly, Disney found a way to manufacture and market fun for every age. Today, Walt Disney's vision has taken his original theme park concept into the international marketplace with Disney World locations in Paris, France; Tokyo, Japan; and Hong Kong.

Chon, Kaye (Kye-Sung) and Thomas A. Maier. *Welcome to Hospitality: An Introduction*, 3rd ed., Delmar, 2010, pp. 349–50.

1. List two transition words in the first paragraph:

   a. _____

   b. _____

2. What type of transition is used in the third paragraph?

   a. definition   c. contrast
   b. classification   d. time order

3. In the fourth paragraph, what two things are being contrasted?

   _____ and

   _____

4. What patterns are used in this essay?

   a. example   c. contrast
   b. classification   d. time order

Interpreting Persuasive Writing

Review Your Understanding of the Two Components of Argument: Point and Support

Unit 9 notes that we are constantly presented with arguments, whether in school, at work, or in our personal lives. Arguments are attempts to influence thinking, attitude, and behavior. Chances are, some of those arguments do just that — they change the way we think.

Strong arguments are composed of a point and support of the point. The point of the argument is the belief or attitude an author wants you to accept. It always raises the question "Why?" The support is included in order to answer the question the point raises. So the support provides the answers to the question "Why?" by providing specific reasons, facts, examples, or other details.

While every point needs support, it has to be the right kind of support. Remember, support has to be relevant and help valid the point.

Apply Your Understanding of the Two Components of Argument: Point and Support

Read the passages below and underline the point in each passage. Then, answer the questions that follow.

Passage 1

1) New studies show that playing video games may actually be good for children. 2) Many positive skills can be learned from playing video games. 3) According to a website developed at Miami University in Ohio, research has been completed that proves that skills such as problem-solving, perseverance, hypothesizing, estimating, critical thinking, resource management, logic, quick thinking, and reasoned judgments can be developed through playing video games. 4) The same research also shows that "video games mimic social structure" and may allow students to develop leadership abilities not normally developed through other types of play. 5) Video gaming is interactive as well, and helps students develop good hand-eye coordination. 6) And children can also develop self-esteem by mastering difficult games, proving to their friends that they have a valuable skill set that is recognizable in their particular peer group.

What sentences above provide support? _____

_____

_____

Is the support presented relevant to the point? Why or why not? _____

_____

_____

_____

_____

What other support could the author of this passage include? _____

_____

_____

_____

Passage 2

1) Although biology provides two distinct and universal sexes, cultures provide almost infinitely varied gender roles. 2) Each man is pretty much like every other man in terms of sex—whether he is upper class or lower class, African American or white, Chinese or Apache. 3) Gender, however, is a different matter. 4) The rights, obligations, dispositions, and activities of the male gender are very different for a Chinese man than for an Apache man. 5) Even within a given culture, gender roles vary by class, race, and subculture. 6) In addition, of course, individuals differ in the way they act out their expected roles: Some males model themselves after Brad Pitt and some after Johnny Depp or Will Smith.

Brinkerhoff, David B., et al. "Chapter 9." *Essentials of Sociology*, 8th ed., Wadsworth, 2011, p. 210.

What sentences above provide support? _____

_____

_____

Is the support presented relevant to the point? Why or why not? _____

_____

_____

_____

_____

What other support could the author of this passage include? _____

_____

_____

_____

_____

Note: *Passages 3 and 4 are parts of the same passage. Therefore, they make up one larger reading.*

Passage 3

1) I happen to agree with the decision not to execute Andrea Yates, the Texas mother convicted of drowning her five children in the bathtub. 2) But I think it's appalling that in so many other cases of capital murder, in Texas and elsewhere, defendants are moved through the system as if on an assembly line, with little or no serious consideration given to possible extenuating circumstances, including mental retardation and severe mental illness. 3) I've written before about Mario Marquez, whose case was one of many in Texas in which the background and mental state of the defendant was not sufficiently considered. 4) Mr. Marquez had an IQ of 65 and was savagely abused as a child. 5) At times his father would beat him with a horsewhip until he passed out. 6) His parents abandoned him to the streets when he was 12. 7) Mr. Marquez was too limited mentally to talk with his lawyer about his case. 8) They talked about animals and the things Mr. Marquez liked to draw. 9) He was executed in 1995.

What sentences above provide support? _____

_____

_____

Is the support presented relevant to the point? Why or why not? _____

_____

_____

_____

_____

What other support could the author of this passage include? _____

_____

_____

_____

_____

Passage 4

10) The death penalty can never be administered consistently with any reasonable degree of fairness and equity. 11) Too many prejudices and preconceived notions are held by the inherently fallible humans who operate the system. 12) And there are too many unknowns when complex issues of culpability arise: Who's insane, or not insane? Who's mentally retarded? Who's lying and who's not? Was it self-defense? Was it an accident? 13) In the court of public opinion, there's no agreement on whether Andrea Yates should even have been convicted. 14) Some conservative commentators, ordinarily hot for the death penalty, have joined others in arguing that she should have been acquitted by reason of insanity. 15) In criminal cases, unanswered and unanswerable questions abound. 16) You can never achieve the kind of certainty that should be required if you're sending defendants to their doom. 17) It is past time to set the death penalty aside.

Adapted from Herbert, Bob. "Deciding Who Will Live." *The New York Times*, 18 Mar. 2002.

What sentences above provide support? _____

_____

_____

Is the support presented relevant to the point? Why or why not? _____

_____

_____

_____

_____

What other support could the author of this passage include? _____

_____

_____

_____

_____

Review Your Understanding of Informed vs. Uninformed Opinions

There are opinions that are more informed than others. Informed opinions are supported by fact, meaning they can be verified. Uninformed opinions cannot be verified or proven because they are based on things other than confirmed fact.

When you are reading, evaluate what kind of evidence is presented. Does the evidence consist of facts and data? If not, then it is likely that the piece is forwarding uninformed opinions. Without concrete evidence or at least an informed opinion, it is often hard to take an author at their word or accept any argument they are trying to make.

Apply Your Understanding of Informed vs. Uninformed Opinions

For each of the longer passages, paraphrase the selection's main point. Then, evaluate the evidence the author offers in support of that main claim. Are the opinions informed or uninformed? Does the evidence seem accurate and adequate? Why or why not? Does each author convince you to agree with his or her main point? Why or why not?

Passage 1

In an interview more than 20 years ago, the great fiction writer Joseph Wambaugh, who was once an LAPD sergeant, complained that the entertainment media trivialized violence by creating what he labeled "cosmetized violence." Wambaugh meant that on television especially, a great deal of violence was acted out in a way that was so unrealistic as to make it appear inconsequential and even romantic. Actors are regularly shot, stabbed, pummeled, and strangled without showing anything remotely approaching what such action does to the human body in real life. He pointed out that this numbs the viewer in a way.

Police dramas are particularly vulnerable to falling into this dynamic. Police programs on television are replete with high-speed automobile chases, prolonged gunfights that approach the intensity of pitched battles, and constant physical altercations between police and citizens. Viewers are left with the idea that police work is not only dangerous but consistently exciting and something akin to ongoing warfare.

Such cosmetized violence socializes viewers into thinking that the consequences of violent behavior are far less horrific than they really are. It desensitizes us all in a way—by suggesting that resorting to violence is not something that should be eschewed or avoided if at all possible. Not only are people desensitized by the type of violence portrayed in this unrealistic way, but also by the amount of violence portrayed on television. One study a number of years ago suggested that the average five-year-old child entering Kindergarten had already seen more than 4,000 people "die" on television.

This type of pretend violence affects the police for several reasons. First, normalizing violence and everyday brutality in this way suggests to young people that violence is romantic and sexy. There is every reason to believe that this increases the amount of violence on the streets of America. This in turn means that there is more violence with which police officers must deal.

Second, television and motion pictures create an image of the average, everyday police officer as a superhuman martial arts expert. Some people, perhaps the more gullible among us, come to expect this from the police. While police officers are given training in the area of "defensive tactics," there are no superhuman police officers out there. None. And the inability of real-life police officers to live up to this imagery can move citizens, once again, to believe that their local police are incompetent.

Finally, police work is not filled with action and violence and confrontation on a minute-by-minute basis. As has been said by many people over the years, a shift out on the street for a police officer often involves "three hours of paper work, four hours of boredom, an hour's worth of action, and three minutes of terror." Even this statement romanticizes police work, since the three minutes of terror is seldom visited upon the average police officer in the average shift.

Perez, Douglas W. "Chapter 6." *Paradoxes of Police Work*, 2nd ed., Delmar, 2011, pp. 110–12.

Main Claim: _____

_____

_____

_____

Evaluation of the evidence: _____

_____

_____

_____

_____

_____

_____

_____

Passage 2

The college experience provides late adolescents or young adults a unique environment that is, to some degree, protected from the larger society within which it exists. Within the sheltered environment of a post-secondary educational facility, a sense of community membership evolves for students who reside in both on-campus and off-campus housing. The institution provides an isolated environment in which there is minimal parental supervision for the most part, but in which students are faced with unique academic, behavioral, interpersonal, developmental, and financial demands. Their ability to adapt is both tested and often rewarded with opportunities that do not exist outside of the postsecondary environment.

The college experience forces the high school graduate to attempt multiple tasks simultaneously: (a) learning to function independently in a challenging academic environment, (b) developing social networks that might prove supportive (or distracting) from the first task, and (c) possibly dealing with the feelings that follow separation from home for extended periods. During this phase of life, young people's relationship with their parents will also evolve, and often areas of conflict are outgrown as parents assume the new role of mentors in young adults' lives. As college students make this transition, they must reexamine their relationship with alcohol and the other drugs of abuse, a process that will continue throughout the college years and that overlaps with the other tasks outlined earlier.

Upon entering college, students begin the process of building a peer relationship support system consistent with their expectations and goals for college. Those students with the strongest motives for attending college are typically more likely to reach out to others with similar values and least likely to abuse alcohol or recreational drugs because this would interfere with their academic goals. This is seen in the fact that although 17.6 percent of young adults have abused an opioid, only 1.9 percent of college students report doing so. There is, however, a subpopulation of undergraduates who turn to alcohol or other drugs as a means of dealing with the pressure to meet academic expectations. Although alcohol or the other recreational drugs might relieve some of the stress and anxiety experienced by these students during the academic years, such substance abuse also can contribute to a vicious cycle of substance abuse related to poor academic performance, increased stress, increased use of chemicals to address that stress, and then further deterioration in academic performance. Johnson (2010) reported, for example, that one-quarter of college students admitted that their alcohol use had caused drinking-related academic problems such as missing classes, poor grades, or failing to keep up with assigned materials.

In contrast to the student population with strong academic goals, some undergraduates find that heavy alcohol use facilitates the establishment of social relationships with other heavy alcohol users and is a strong motivating factor for continued heavy alcohol use. Unfortunately, there is an inverse relationship between the individuals' level of alcohol use and academic performance, as many students discover to their dismay.

Doweiko, Harold E. *Concepts of Chemical Dependency*, 8th ed., Cengage Learning, 2012.

Main Claim: _____

_____

_____

_____

Evaluation of the evidence: _____

_____

_____

_____

_____

_____

_____

_____

_____

_____

Review Your Understanding of Common Persuasion Signal Words and Transitions

There are many common signal words and transitional phrases for persuasive writing. They often appear with, within, or in order to introduce the passage's support. By default then, if you are able to locate the signal words or transitional phrases, you are also able to identify the author's provided evidence.

Here are some examples of signal words and transitions:

Type of Signal Word or Transition	Examples
Phrases Used to Introduce	In my opinion, I believe, It is my belief that, There is no double that, From my point of view, I question whether, I agree/disagree with, I maintain that, It seems to me
Phrases Used to Conclude	For the reasons above, In short, In brief, As you can see, To be sure, Undoubtedly, As I have noted, Without a doubt, In any case, In other words, Obviously, Summarizing, Unquestionably, In any event
Used to Support Point through Evidence	First, Furthermore, Equally important, Besides, Further, Second, In addition, In the first place, Next, Again, Third, Also, Likewise, Moreover, Similarly, Finally, Last
Used to Introduce Evidence	For example, For instance, As evidence, In support of this, In fact
Used to Counter a Point	I realize, I understand you, Even though, But, Yet, However, Although, I doubt, Some people, I question, It may be, Nevertheless, On the contrary, On the other hand

Apply Your Understanding of Common Persuasion Signal Words and Transitions

Read this persuasive essay on writing. As you read, underline the signal words and phrases and transitions that you encounter. Then, discuss how the transition words provide clues that suggest this is a persuasive essay.

Where has the joy of writing gone and how do we get it back for our children?

There is a clear link between students being engaged with writing and the quality of literacy outcomes. Students' willingness to write can be promoted by making writing more enjoyable and meaningful to young people, with authentic connections to their lives.

Research in English and literacy education consistently shows when teachers are given the scope to tap into students' interests, they can produce work of high quality. To increase students' enjoyment of writing, more time could be given to creative forms of writing such as poetry, song lyrics, short scripts, personal memoirs and comic pieces, and combinations of different types of texts with visual materials in multimodal and digital composition.

It's important for children's literacy for them to fall in love with writing. We now have a rich body of research and toolkits that support teachers in writing instruction. Building on good writing instruction, it's also important for writing to be an activity done for intrinsic purposes such as pleasure. The Australian Association for the Teaching of English asserts the importance of this goal. Writing is more than work for achieving an outcome. It's identity work. In the enjoyment of writing, student writers can find themselves and discover the power of language. Powerful literacy skills can be gained in this discovery, with lifelong implications.

Despite the link between writing for enjoyment and positive literacy results, there is accumulating evidence that writing instruction in schools is becoming limited. The current focus on forms of writing tested in standardized formats, such as tests like NAPLAN and PIRLS, puts pressure on teachers and schools to narrow writing instruction. Typically, this would mean a focus on producing essays, persuasive pieces, reports, recounts, descriptive writing and procedural texts.

In NSW, Geoff Masters, the CEO of the Australian Council for Educational Research (ACER), is overseeing a comprehensive review of that state's curriculum. He has already noted teachers and school leaders are bound by an inflexible curriculum. This includes approaches to writing and literacy that focus too heavily on prescribed functional texts. Other research by ACER suggests the need for more openness and innovation in teaching writing.

Teachers are committed to improving their students' writing, given the emphasis in class on assessment of writing by NAPLAN and other international tests. But they also need to feel they can allow more time for unstructured or personal writing that promotes creative writing identities for students.

A focus on testing can stifle pleasure in writing. For example, teaching multimodal composition (where two or more modes such as written language, spoken language, visual or audio are combined) and writing designed for performance alongside mandated forms of writing (such as persuasive, narrative or instructional writing) would allow students to develop important skills in writing that reflect the emerging digital world and a range of necessary literacy competencies.

The key to promoting the effective writing skills needed by students is to be found in making writing engaging, meaningful and pleasurable. Every opportunity should be taken to open up the possibilities of writing for students so they want to do it and see its relevance to their lives. There also needs to be a shift in the current policy and assessment emphasis on specific outcomes to one which empowers teachers to promote writing to learn and writing for enjoyment.

What can teachers and parents do at home and at school to foster an enjoyment of writing? Teachers can promote enjoyable writing with meaningful writing environments. Teachers can open up writing for pleasure in their classrooms, either as a core activity or as an extension after other work is completed. There can be a special class time to share or perform creative and personal writing and for other students to comment about it. Teachers can also write alongside students to model good writing behaviors. Schools can promote writing clubs where students can write together, share their writing and even self-publish it in online forums and blogs.

Parents can encourage children to write for pleasure, not just for school work. For example, having a personal diary or journal, and in it writing about life, what interests them, or for imagining, storytelling and wondering.

Creely, Edwin and Diamond Fleur. "**Where Has the Joy of Writing Gone and How Do We Get It Back for Our Children?**" *The Conversation*, **21 Nov. 2018.** https://theconversation.com/where-has-the-joy-of-writing-gone-and-how-do-we-get-it-back-for-our-children-101900.

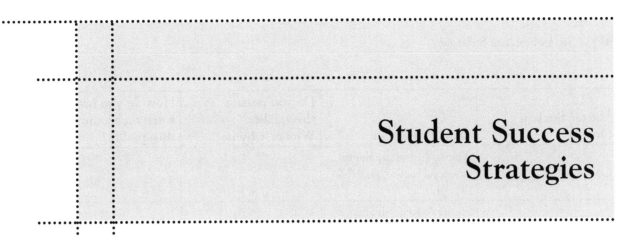

Student Success Strategies

Review Your Understanding of Becoming a Master Student

All of us have at least one thing we feel we are very good or gifted at. This skill may be in your personal life, in regard to athletics, or related to your academic journey. Think about your gift. Would you consider yourself a master at it yet? Becoming a master at something brings a sense of satisfaction, wellbeing, and timeliness – feelings we all desire and strive toward. Maybe you do not feel your gift is related to school at all. That's okay…the truth is, you already possess some of the same qualities that master students share. The good news? You can acquire more.

Apply Your Understanding of Becoming a Master Student

In the Unit, you were provided with a list of master student qualities. While this list is not complete, it does provide you with an idea of qualities master students share. In the table below, some of the master student qualities are listed. By filling out the table, you can start to identify your path to becoming a master student.

First, answer if you possess the common master student quality, explaining why or why not. Then, answer how you plan to work on that skillset in the future. You may write directly in the boxes provided or on another sheet a paper.

Master Student Quality	Short Definition	Do you possess this quality? Why or why not?	How do you plan to work on acquiring this quality?
Inquisitive	Curious about everything; asks questions		
Able to Focus	Sees world as new or a place of amazement		
Willing to Change	Embraces new ideas and strategies if they mean success		
Able to Organize and Sort	Can sift through a lot of information easily		

65

Master Student Quality	Short Definition	Do you possess this quality? Why or why not?	How do you plan to work on acquiring this quality?
Competent	Able to learn fast, almost as second nature, and able to apply		
Joyful	Positive about self and world around you		
Able to Suspend Judgment	Can let go of opinions and positions when necessary		
Energetic	Determined, persistent, and applies energy to all you do		
Well	Healthy, all the way around		
Intuitive	Has gut instincts that cannot be explained		
Optimistic	Can choose response to any circumstance		
Self-directed	Able to push self to next level of excellence		
Willing to Work	Works with intensity in order to be successful		

Review Your Understanding of Ways to Change a Habit

Changing a habit is not easy, but it can be done. When thinking about future success, or failure, you may want to focus on habits you have right now. Are your current habits likely to set you up for success or failure? If you have a habit that limits you in some way, or has the potential to do so in the future, it is time to take on the task of changing it. The unit discussed a few ways to do just that:

1) Start Small

2) Rehearse the New Habit

3) Trigger the Habit

4) Practice the New Habit

5) Give it Time

In his book, *The Power of Habit*, Charles Duhigg explains that all habits have three elements:

- **Routine.** This is a behavior that we repeat, usually without thinking. Examples are taking a second helping at dinner, biting fingernails, or automatically hitting the snooze button when the alarm goes off in the morning.

- **Cue.** Also known as a *trigger*, this is an event that occurs right before we perform the routine. It might be an internal event, such as a change in mood. Or it could be an external event, such as seeing an advertisement that triggers food cravings.
- **Reward.** This is the payoff for the routine—usually a feeling of pleasure or a reduction in stress.

Taken together, these elements form a habit loop: You perceive a *cue* and then perform a *routine* in order to get a *reward*.

Apply Your Understanding of Ways to Change a Habit

Use this exercise to test Duhigg's ideas for yourself. There are 5 steps to follow below. Read each prompt and then respond on the lines or in the table provided.

Step 1: Identify your current routine.
Describe the habit that you want to change. Refer to a specific behavior that anyone could observe—preferably a physical, visible action that you perform every day.

I discovered that the habit I want to change is . . .

_____

_____

_____

_____

Step 2: Identify the cue.
Next, think about what takes place immediately before you perform the routine. For instance, drinking a cup of coffee (cue) might trigger the urge to eat a cookie (routine).

I discovered that the cue for the behavior I described is . . .

_____

_____

_____

_____

Step 3: Identify the reward.
Now for the "goodie." Reflect on the reward you get from your routine. Do you gain a distraction from discomfort? A pleasant sensation in your body? A chance to socialize with friends or coworkers? Describe the details.

I discovered that my reward for my current routine is . . .

_____

_____

_____

_____

Step 4: Choose a new routine.

Now choose a different routine that you can perform in response to the cue. The challenge is to choose a behavior that offers a reward with as few disadvantages as possible. Instead of eating a whole cookie, for example, you could break off just one small section and eat it slowly, with full attention. This would allow you to experience a familiar pleasure with a fraction of the calories. Describe your new routine.

The new routine that I intend to do is . . .

_____

_____

_____

_____

Step 5: Create a visual summary of your experience with habit change.

After practicing your new routine for at least seven days, fill in the following chart to summarize what you did. Use the "Notes" column to describe what you learned, including anything that surprised you, consequences of the new routine, and things that will be useful to remember when you plan habit changes in the future.

Current Routine	Cue	Reward	New Routine	Notes

Review Your Understanding of Trigger the Habit

To be more likely to change a behavior or habit, it is smart to connect the new one, or what you wish to change, to something you do already with consistency. For example, let's pretend you are working on your health.

Scenario: Right now, you always eat breakfast out, while on-the-go. You know this is a bad habit because it costs more money and because the things you order are not as healthy as what you can eat or make at home. Since always on the go, breakfast is usually rushed so it does not digest well. So, you need a new habit: to make and eat breakfast at home.

- Behavior to Change: I eat breakfast out, while on-the-go.
- New Habit: Make and eat breakfast at home.
- Something Already Done Consistently: Take the dog out and feed her breakfast before taking a shower.
- Trigger: Take the dog out.
- Plan New Habit Statement: After I take the dog out, I will make and eat breakfast.

Apply Your Understanding of Trigger the Habit

As mentioned in the unit, B.J. Fogg recommends using new habit statements that work like this: After I ＿＿＿＿＿ (this is your consistent), I will ＿＿＿＿＿ (this is your new habit). Now, it is your time to plan for some new habits.
Using the template below, plan five potential new habits.

1. Behavior to Change: ＿＿＿＿＿＿＿＿＿＿＿＿＿＿＿＿＿＿＿＿

   New Habit: ＿＿＿＿＿＿＿＿＿＿＿＿＿＿＿＿＿＿＿＿＿＿

   Something Already Done Consistently: ＿＿＿＿＿＿＿＿＿＿＿

   ＿＿＿＿＿＿＿＿＿＿＿＿＿＿＿＿＿＿＿＿＿＿＿＿＿＿＿＿

   Trigger: ＿＿＿＿＿＿＿＿＿＿＿＿＿＿＿＿＿＿＿＿＿＿＿＿

   After I ＿＿＿＿＿＿＿＿＿＿＿＿＿＿＿＿＿＿＿＿＿＿＿＿,

   I will ＿＿＿＿＿＿＿＿＿＿＿＿＿＿＿＿＿＿＿＿＿＿＿＿＿.

2. Behavior to Change: ＿＿＿＿＿＿＿＿＿＿＿＿＿＿＿＿＿＿＿

   New Habit: ＿＿＿＿＿＿＿＿＿＿＿＿＿＿＿＿＿＿＿＿＿＿

   Something Already Done Consistently: ＿＿＿＿＿＿＿＿＿＿＿

   ＿＿＿＿＿＿＿＿＿＿＿＿＿＿＿＿＿＿＿＿＿＿＿＿＿＿＿＿

Trigger: _____

After I _____,

I will _____.

3. Behavior to Change: _____

New Habit: _____

Something Already Done Consistently: _____

_____

Trigger: _____

After I _____,

I will _____.

4. Behavior to Change: _____

New Habit: _____

Something Already Done Consistently: _____

_____

Trigger: _____

After I _____,

I will _____.

5. Behavior to Change: _____

New Habit: _____

Something Already Done Consistently: _____

_____

Trigger: _____

After I _____,

I will _____.

Part 2

Applying Reading Strategies Across the Curriculum

Short Passages

Below are six passages taken from textbooks from different disciplines: Communications, Psychology, Political Science, Sociology, Health, and History. Read each passage and answer the accompanying questions.

Passage 1: Communications

Interviews can be more or less formal. In highly formal interviews, participants tend to stay closely within social and professional roles. They do little to acknowledge each other as unique individuals. Instead, the interviewer acts as the potential employer, the corrective supervisor, or whatever role is pertinent to the type of interview being conducted. The interviewee also acts from a defined role: prospective employee, repentant subordinate, and so forth. The content of highly formal interviews tends to follow a standard format, often one that the interviewer has written to structure the interaction. Nonverbal communication provides further clues to formality: clothes, a formal meeting room, stilted postures, and a stiff handshake are all signs of formality.

In contrast, informal interviews are more relaxed, personal, and flexible. The interviewer attempts to engage the interviewee as an individual, not just a person in a general role. In turn, the interviewee tends to communicate with the interviewer in more individualistic ways. Typically, informal interviews aren't as rigidly structured as formal interviews. The interviewer may have a list of standard topics (either memorized or written down), but those provide only guidelines, not a **straightjacket** for communication. Either participant may introduce unusual topics, and they may devote more time than planned to issues that arise. Informal interviews often include nonverbal cues such as smiling, relaxed postures, casual surroundings, and informal dress.

Wood, Julia T. *Communication in Our Lives*, 3rd ed., Wadsworth, 2003, p. 332.

1. What is the main idea of the passage?

   _____

   _____

   _____

   _____

2. What pattern of organization is used in the passage?

    _____

    _____

3. According to the article, which of the following is NOT true about informal interviews?

    _____

    _____

    _____

    _____

4. What is the primary purpose of the passage?

    _____

    _____

    _____

    _____

5. What does the word **straightjacket** mean in the second paragraph?

    _____

    _____

6. Identify the relationship between the following sentences from the first paragraph.

    "Instead, the interviewer acts as the potential employer, the corrective supervisor, or whatever role is pertinent to the type of interview being conducted." "The interviewee also acts from a defined role: prospective employee, repentant subordinate, and so forth."

    _____

    _____

    _____

    _____

Passage 2: Psychology

Studies show **conclusively** that if large groups of children watch a great deal of televised violence, they will be more prone to behave aggressively. In other words, not all children will become more aggressive, but many will. Especially during adolescence, viewing lots of violence on television is associated with actual increases in aggression against others. It's little wonder that a large panel of medical and psychological experts recently concluded that media violence is a serious threat to public health.

It is fair to say, then, that televised violence causes aggression in viewers, especially children? Fortunately, that would be an exaggeration. Televised violence can make aggression more *likely*, but it does not invariably "cause" it to occur for any given child. Many other factors affect the chances that hostile thoughts will be turned into actions. Among children, one such factor is the extent to which a child identifies with aggressive characters. That's why it is so sad to find TV heroes behaving aggressively, as well as villains.

A case in point is the popular Power Rangers TV programs for children. In each episode, the Power Rangers "morph" into superheroes who use karate and other violent actions to conquer monsters. After watching an episode of the Power Rangers, a group of 7-year-old children committed seven times more aggressive acts than a control group that didn't watch. The aggressive children hit, kicked, and karate-chopped their peers, often directly imitating the Power Rangers. Younger children, in particular, are more likely to be influenced by such programs because they don't fully recognize that the characters and stories are fantasies.

Youngsters who believe that aggression is an acceptable way to solve problems, who believe that TV violence is realistic, and who identify with TV characters are more likely to copy televised aggression. In view of such findings, it is understandable that Canada, Norway, and Switzerland have restricted the amount of permissible violence on television. Should all countries do the same?

Coon, Dennis. *Introduction to Psychology*, 10th ed., Wadsworth, 2004, pp. 321–22.

1. What is the main idea of the passage?

   _____

   _____

   _____

   _____

2. As an example, what is the television show *Power Rangers* used to demonstrate in the passage?

   _____

   _____

   _____

   _____

3. According to the passage, why are young children more strongly influenced by violent programs?

   _____

   _____

   _____

   _____

4. Is the last sentence of the first paragraph ("It's little wonder that...) fact or opinion? Provide an explanation of your answer.

    _____

    _____

    _____

    _____

5. In the first paragraph, what does the word **conclusively** mean?

    _____

    _____

    _____

    _____

6. Write a summary of the passage.

    _____

    _____

    _____

    _____

    _____

    _____

    _____

    _____

Passage 3: Political Science

For some Americans, the political concepts that are set forth in the Declaration of Independence—particularly the concept of equality—have become standards by which American institutions should be measured. For example, as you will see, the Constitution did not allow for equal treatment for many Americans, including African Americans (who were not considered citizens) and women. The **disparity** between the declaration's promise of equality and the Constitution's unequal treatment of Americans set the example for future conflicts over the issue of equality.

Neither Thomas Jefferson nor the framers of the Constitution interpreted the word *equality* to mean equal income. Rather, they envisioned a nation in which all citizens had what we would now call equal opportunity. Equal opportunity promotes other American ideals, such as individualism and self-reliance. It also often leads to a **meritocracy** based on individual talent and effort. Those who have the advantage of more education, more money to invest in an enterprise, greater talent, and higher levels of energy will have a competitive edge and come out the winners.

In recent times, some people have been unwilling to accept the results of simple equality of opportunity if it creates a gross maldistribution of wealth. Some have argued that the founders, who lived in a largely agrarian economy, could not have envisioned the huge disparities in income in an industrial age and certainly would not have thought them consistent with democratic government. Some reformers have thus backed the creation of a welfare safety net by which the government protects and promotes the economic security of its citizens. Other reformers have tried to level the playing field through programs known as "affirmative action." These programs give preferences to minorities and other groups to make up for past discrimination. Those who favor affirmative action views its opponents as heartless individualists, who would let other Americans remain in poverty because they lack the talent, luck, or education to rise above it. Opponents of affirmative action argue that such programs perpetuate unequal treatment and emphasize racial divisions in society.

Sidlow, Edward and Beth Henschen. *America at Odds*, 4th ed., Wadsworth, 2004, p. 27.

1. In the first paragraph, what does the word **disparity** mean?

   _____

   _____

2. According to the passage, what did the writers of the Constitution consider "equality" to mean?

   _____

   _____

   _____

   _____

3. How is the first sentence of the second paragraph ("Neither Thomas Jefferson nor the framers of the Constitution...") related to the second sentence of the paragraph ("Rather, they envisioned a nation...")? Is it an example, definition, contrast, addition, etc.?

   _____

   _____

   _____

   _____

4. What is the overall pattern of organization used in the passage? How do you know? Provide evidence of the pattern.

   _____

   _____

   _____

   _____

5. In the second paragraph, what is the meaning of **meritocracy**? Once you have noted the
    meaning, write an original sentence in which you use the term.

    _____

    _____

    _____

    _____

    _____

Passage 4: Sociology

The Industrial Revolution refers to the social and economic changes that occurred when machines
and factories, rather than human labor, became the dominant mode for the production of goods.
Industrialization occurred in the United States during the early and mid-1800s and represents one
of the most profound influences on the family.

Before industrialization, families functioned as an economic unit that produced goods and services for its own consumption. Parents and children worked together in or near the home to meet
the survival needs of the family. As the United States became industrialized, more men and women
left the home to sell their labor for wages. The family was no longer a self-sufficient unit that
determined its work hours. Rather, employers determined where and when family members would
work. Whereas children in pre-industrialized America worked on farms and contributed to the economic survival of the family, children in industrialized America became economic liabilities rather
than assets. Child labor laws and **mandatory** education removed children from the labor force and
lengthened their dependence on parental support. Eventually, both parents had to work away from
the home to support their children. The dual-income family had begun.

During the Industrial Revolution, urbanization occurred as cities were built around factories
and families moved to the city to work in the factories. Living space in cities was crowded and
expensive, which contributed to a decline in the birthrate and to smaller families.

The development of transportation systems during the Industrial Revolution made it possible
for family members to travel to work sites away from the home and to move away from extended
kin. With increased mobility, many extended families became separated into smaller nuclear family
units consisting of parents and their children. As a result of parents' leaving the home to earn wages
and the absence of extended kin in or near the family household, children had less adult supervision and moral guidance. Unsupervised children roamed the streets, increasing the potential for
crime and delinquency.

Knox, David and Caroline Schacht. *Choices in Relationships: An Introduction to Marriage and the Family*, 7th ed., Thomson
Learning, 2002, p. 16.

1. What is the main idea of the passage?

    _____

    _____

    _____

    _____

2. In the second paragraph, what does the word **mandatory** mean?

    _____

    _____

    _____

3. According to the passage, what conditions brought about the two-income family?

    _____

    _____

    _____

    _____

4. What is the pattern of organization used in the third paragraph of the passage? How do you
    know this? Provide evidence of this pattern.

    _____

    _____

    _____

    _____

5. What can you conclude from this passage?

    _____

    _____

    _____

    _____

Passage 5: Health

Obesity generally is defined as an accumulation of fat (adipose tissue) beyond what is considered
normal for a person's age, sex, and body type. In today's society obesity is considered a disease, not a
moral failing. It occurs when energy intake exceeds the amount of energy expended over time. Only
in a small minority of cases is obesity caused by such illnesses as hypothyroidism, or the result of
taking medications, such as steroids, that can cause weight gain.

The more a person weighs, the more blood vessels the body needs to circulate blood throughout the body. The heart takes on a heavy burden as it has to pump harder to force the blood flow through so many vessels. As a result, the heart grows in size and blood pressure tends to rise. Obesity is also a factor in osteoarthritis (because of the extra weight placed on the joints), gout, bone and joint diseases (including ruptured intervertebral discs), varicose veins, respiratory ailments, gallbladder disease, complications during pregnancy and delivery, and higher accidental death rate.

Obesity can alter hormone levels, affect immune function, and cause impotence in men and reproductive problems in women. Women who are 30% overweight are twice as likely to die of endometrial cancer, and those who are 40% overweight have four times the risk. Obese women also are more likely to incur cancers of the breast, cervix, ovaries, and gallbladder. Obese men are more likely to develop cancers of the rectum, colon, esophagus, bladder, pancreas, stomach, and prostate.

Obesity can also cause psychological problems. Sufferers are associated with laziness, failure, or inadequate willpower. As a result, overweight men and women blame themselves for being heavy, thus causing feelings of guilt and depression.

Scientific evidence has found an association between BMI (body-mass index) and higher death rates. However, the relative risk of being heavy declines with age. Some researchers have found that data linking overweight and death are inconclusive, while other researchers have found that losing weight may be riskier than dangers posed by extra pounds. Some researchers counter that overweight indirectly contributes to over 300,000 deaths a year.

A poll by Shape Up America found that 78% of overweight or obese adults have abandoned dieting as a means of losing weight. Diets do not teach people how to eat properly. They merely restrict food intake temporarily, so when the diet ends, weight gain resumes.

Floyd, Patricia A., et al. *Personal Health*, 3rd ed., Brooks-Cole, 2012, pp. 320–21.

1. What is the main idea of the passage?

   _____

   _____

   _____

   _____

2. Cite at least two supporting ideas/details from the passage.

   _____

   _____

   _____

   _____

3. What is the pattern of organization used in this passage? How do you know this? Provide evidence of the pattern.

   _____

   _____

   _____

   _____

4. According to the passage, why does dieting not result in permanent weight loss?

   _____

   _____

   _____

   _____

5. What type of evidence is used in the passage? Provide examples of each type of evidence.

   _____

   _____

   _____

   _____

Passage 6: History

The choice of the Potomac for the nation's capital was controversial. While everyone agreed that a central location was necessary, regional interests surfaced as congressmen recognized its potential economic and political benefits. They also debated the question of the temporary capital. Should New York City or Philadelphia host the federal government until the permanent site was ready? The complicated negotiations over funding and assumption resulted in moving the temporary capital from New York to Philadelphia as well as locating the new city on the Potomac.

President Washington and his fellow Virginians supervised the development of the capital. The Residence Act of 1790 gave the president authority to select a ten-mile square location somewhere along the Potomac; he chose the land on both sides of the river that included Alexandria, Virginia, and Georgetown, Maryland. The federal city would be built in neither of those towns, but on open land on the east bank of the river. Washington appointed a surveyor, three commissioners to manage the project, and Pierre Charles L'Enfant to design the layout of the capital and its major buildings. L'Enfant's **grandiose** street plan and Greek and Roman architecture expressed an exalted vision of the republic. The commissioners named the federal city "Washington" and the entire district "Columbia."

The president expected to finance construction by selling lots in the capital, thinking that land prices would skyrocket as citizens valued **proximity** to the seat of government. Instead, land sold poorly and lack of money undermined the project. At one of the failed auctions, even the participation of the president and a parade of two brass bands and an artillery troop could not foster sales. When the commissioners suspended construction temporarily for insufficient funds, L'Enfant protested and was fired. His plan for grand boulevards, public squares, fountains, and imposing buildings was retained, but its execution would wait. For a decade the enterprise limped along, saved by grants from Maryland and Virginia. In 1800, when the government moved to Washington, the president's mansion was still unfinished and only one wing of the Capitol had been built.

Ayers, Edward L., et al. American Passages: A History of the United States, 2nd ed., Wadsworth, 2006, p. 197.

1. What is the main idea of the passage?

    _____

    _____

    _____

    _____

2. What is the main purpose of the passage?

    _____

    _____

    _____

    _____

3. What is the pattern of organization used in the third paragraph? Provide evidence of this pattern.

    _____

    _____

    _____

    _____

4. In the second paragraph, what does the word **grandiose** mean?

    _____

    _____

    _____

    _____

5. According to the passage, why was L'Enfant fired?

    _____

    _____

    _____

    _____

Short Textbook Excerpts

Below are four short textbook excerpts from a variety of disciplines, including Management, Psychology, Chemistry, and the Humanities. Read each excerpt, and then answer the questions.

Management: "Diversity"

Actively read the excerpt from a management textbook that follows, and then answer the questions below.

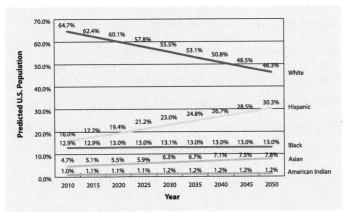

Exhibit 12.1

Percent of the Projected Population by Race and Hispanic Origin for the United States: 2010 to 2050

Note: The original race data from Census 2000 are modified to eliminate the "some other race" category. This modification is used for all Census Bureau projections products and is explained in the document entitled "Modified Race Data Summary File Technical Documentation and ASCII Layout" that can be found on the Census Bureau website at http://www.census.gov/popest/archives/files/MRSF-01-US1.html.
Sources: Population Division, U.S. Census Bureau, August 14, 2008; "Percent of the Projected Population by Race and Hispanic Origin for the United States: 2008 to 2050," U.S. Census Bureau, 14 August 2008, available at http://www.census.gov/population/www/projections/tablesandcharts/table_4.xls [accessed 4 November 2009].

1 Diversity: Differences That Matter

You'll begin your exploration of diversity by learning **1.1 that diversity is not affirmative action** and **1.2 how to build a business case for diversity.**

1.1 Diversity Is Not Affirmative Action

A common misconception is that workplace diversity and affirmative action are the same, yet these concepts differ in several critical ways, including their purpose, how they are practiced, and the reactions they produce. To start with, **affirmative action** refers to purposeful steps taken by an organization to create employment opportunities for minorities and women.[6] By contrast, diversity exists in organizations when there is a variety of demographic, cultural, and personal differences among the people who work there and the customers

> **Affirmative action**
> purposeful steps taken by an organization to create employment opportunities for minorities and women

who do business there. So, one key difference is that affirmative action is more narrowly focused on demographics such as sex and race, while diversity has a broader focus that includes demographic, cultural, and personal differences. A second difference is that affirmative action is a policy for actively creating diversity, but diversity can exist even if organizations don't take purposeful steps to create it. For example, Longo Toyota achieved a high level of diversity without having a formal affirmative action program. Likewise, a local restaurant located near a university in a major city is likely to have a more diverse group of employees than one located in a small town. Affirmative action does not guarantee diversity. An organization can create employment opportunities for women and minorities yet not have a diverse work force.

A third important difference is that affirmative action is required by law for private employers with 50 or more employees while diversity is not. Affirmative action originated with Executive Order 11246 (https://www.dol.gov/ofccp/regs/compliance/aa.htm) but is also related to the 1964 Civil Rights Act, which bans discrimination in voting, public places, federal government programs, federally supported public education, and employment. Title VII of the Civil Rights Act (http://www.eeoc.gov/laws/statutes/titlevii.cfm) requires that workers have equal employment opportunities when being hired or promoted. More specifically, Title VII prohibits companies from discriminating in their employment practices on the basis of race, color, religion, sex, or national origin. Title VII also created the Equal Employment Opportunity Commission, or EEOC (http://www.eeoc.gov), to administer these laws. By contrast, there is no federal law or agency to oversee diversity. Organizations that pursue diversity goals do so voluntarily.

1. What is the topic of this excerpt?

    a. Economics

    b. Bicycles

    c. Diversity

    d. Affirmative action

2. How many key terms are highlighted and defined in this section?

    a. One

    b. Three

    c. Five

    d. Seven

3. Which of the following learning objectives corresponds to this section?

    a. Explain diversity.

    b. Discuss the differences between the terms *diversity* and *affirmative action*.

    c. List the steps involved in bringing forth an affirmative action lawsuit.

    d. Discuss why people may or may not be qualified for a particular job.

4. What is the purpose of the graph that precedes the section on diversity?

    a. To show how the Hispanic population is staying the same in terms of number.

    b. To show the projected population by race and Hispanic origin from the years 2010 to 2050.

    c. To show the impact of race on the Census.

    d. To show how diverse the United States is.

The following sentences appear in the chapter. Circle the letter of the BEST meaning for each italicized word.

5. "By contrast, diversity exists in organizations when there is a variety of *demographic*, cultural, and personal differences among the people...."

    a. Parts of a population

    b. Opinions

    c. Opposites

    d. Things prone to change

6. "... but diversity can exist even if organizations don't take *purposeful* steps to create it...."

    a. Indeterminate

    b. Deliberate

    c. Wise

    d. Cultural

7. "Organizations that pursue diversity goals do so *voluntarily*."

    a. Willingly

    b. Without fear

    c. Unwittingly

    d. Technologically

For each of the following review questions, write your answer on the blanks provided.

8. Explain how workplace diversity and affirmative action are different.

   _____

   _____

   _____

   _____

   _____

9. Explain the purpose of Executive Order 11246 and how it relates to the 1964 Civil Rights Act.

   _____

   _____

   _____

   _____

   _____

10. What is Title VII and how does it affect hiring practices, if at all, in corporations?

   _____

   _____

   _____

   _____

   _____

Psychology: "Stress and Stressors"

Actively read the excerpt from a psychology textbook, and then answer the questions that follow.

1. Before you actively read this excerpt, transform the section heading into a question and write it here.

   _____

   _____

   _____

   _____

   _____

This table shows five of the leading causes of death in the United States today, along with behavioral factors that contribute to their development.

table 13.1
Lifestyle Behaviors That Affect the Leading Causes of Death in the United States

Cause of Death	Contributing Behavioral Factor				
	Alcohol	Smoking	Diet	Exercise	Stress
Heart disease	x	x	x	x	x
Cancer	x	x	x		?
Stroke	x	x	x	?	?
Lung disease		x			
Accidents and Injury	x	x			x

Source: Data from USDHHS (1990); Centers for Disease Control and Prevention (1999a).

Running for Your Life   Health psychologists have developed programs to help people increase exercise, stop smoking, eat healthier diets, and make other lifestyle changes that lower their risk of illness and death. They have even helped to insure community blood supplies by finding ways to make blood donation less stressful (Bonk, France, & Taylor, 2001).

century, the major causes of illness and death in the United States and Canada were acute infectious diseases, such as influenza, tuberculosis, and pneumonia. With these afflictions now less threatening, chronic illnesses—such as coronary heart disease, cancer, and diabetes—have joined accidents and injuries as the leading causes of disability and death (Guyer et al., 2000). Further, psychological, lifestyle, and environmental factors play substantial roles in determining whether a person will fall victim to these modern-day killers (Taylor, 1999). For example, lifestyle choices, such as whether a person smokes, affect the risk for the five leading causes of death for men and women in the United States (D'Agostino et al., 2001; Lichtenstein et al., 2000; see Table 13.1). Further, the psychological and behavioral factors that contribute to these illnesses can be altered by psychological interventions, including programs that promote nonsmoking and low-fat diets. As many as half of all deaths in the United States are due to potentially preventable lifestyle behaviors (National Cancer Institute, 1994).

Health psychologists have been active in helping people understand the role they can play in controlling their own health and life expectancy (Baum, Revenson, & Singer, 2001). For example, they have promoted early detection of disease by educating people about the warning signs of cancer, heart disease, and other serious illnesses and encouraging them to seek medical attention while lifesaving treatment is still possible. Health psychologists also study, and help people to understand, the role played by stress in physical health and illness.

Stress and Stressors

You have probably heard that death and taxes are the only two things you can be sure of in life. If there is a third, it must surely be stress. Stress is basic to life—no matter how wealthy, powerful, attractive, or happy you might be. It comes in many forms—a difficult exam, an automobile accident, waiting in a long line, a day on which everything goes wrong. Mild stress can be stimulating, motivating, and sometimes desirable. But as it becomes more severe, stress can bring on physical, psychological, and behavioral problems.

Stress is the negative emotional and physiological process that occurs as individuals try to adjust to or deal with **stressors**, which are environmental circumstances that disrupt, or threaten to disrupt, individuals' daily functioning and cause

stress   The process of adjusting to circumstances that disrupt, or threaten to disrupt, a person's equilibrium.

stressors   Events or situations to which people must adjust.

figure 13.1

The Process of Stress

Stressful events, people's reactions to those events, and interactions between people and the situations they face are all important components of stress. Notice the two-way relationships in the stress process. For example, if a person has effective coping skills, stress responses will be less severe. Having milder stress responses will act as a "reward" that will strengthen those skills. Further, as coping skills (such as refusing unreasonable demands) improve, certain stressors (such as a boss's unreasonable demands) may become less frequent.

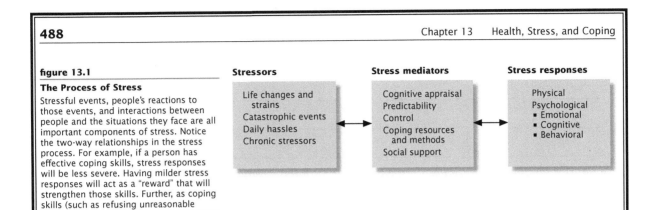

people to make adjustments (Taylor, 1999). In other words, stress involves a *transaction* between people and their environment. Figure 13.1 lists the main types of stressors and illustrates that when confronted by stressors, people respond physically (e.g., with nervousness, nausea, and fatigue), as well as psychologically.

As also shown in Figure 13.1, the transaction between people and their environment can be influenced by *stress mediators*, which include such variables as the extent to which people can predict and control their stressors, how they interpret the threat involved, the social support they get, and their stress-coping skills. (We discuss these mediators in greater detail later.) So stress is not a specific event but a *process* in which the nature and intensity of stress responses depend to a large degree on factors such as the way people think about stressors and the skills and resources they have to cope with them.

For humans, most stressors have both physical and psychological components. Students, for example, are challenged by psychological demands to do well in their courses, as well as by the physical fatigue that can result from a heavy load of classes, combined perhaps with a job and family responsibilities. Similarly, for victims of arthritis, AIDS, and other chronic illnesses, physical pain is accompanied by worry and other forms of psychological distress (Melzack, 1973; Salovey et al., 1992). Here, we focus on psychological stressors, which can stimulate some of the same physiological responses as physical stressors (Cacioppo et al., 1995).

Psychological Stressors

Any event that forces people to accommodate or change can be a psychological stressor. Accordingly, even pleasant events can be stressful (Brown & McGill, 1989). For example, the increased salary and status associated with a promotion may be desirable, but the upgrade usually brings new pressures as well (Schaubroeck, Jones, & Xie, 2001). Similarly, people often feel exhausted after a vacation. Still, it is typically negative events that have the most adverse psychological and physical effects (Kessler, 1997). These circumstances include catastrophic events, life changes and strains, chronic stressors, and daily hassles (Baum, Gatchel, & Krantz, 1997).

Catastrophic events are sudden, unexpected, potentially life-threatening experiences or traumas, such as physical or sexual assault, military combat, natural disasters, terrorist attacks, and accidents. *Life changes* and *strains* include divorce, illness in the family, difficulties at work, moving to a new place, and other circumstances that create demands to which people must adjust (Price, 1992; see Table 13.2). *Chronic stressors*—those that continue over a long period of time—include circumstances such as living near a noisy airport, having a serious illness, being unable to earn a decent living, residing in a high-crime neighborhood, being the victim of discrimination, and even enduring years of academic pressure (Evans, Hygge, & Bullinger, 1995; Levenstein, Smith, & Kaplan, 2001). *Daily hassles* include irritations, pressures, and annoyances that might not be significant stressors by themselves but whose cumulative effects can be significant (Evans & Johnson, 2000).

2. What technique did you use to mark the answers to the question as you read? Did you underline answers? Highlight them? Did you take notes in the margins?

_____

_____

_____

_____

_____

The following sentences appear in the chapter. Circle the letter of the BEST meaning for each italicized word.

3. "Stress is the negative emotional and *physiological* process that occurs as individuals try to adjust to or deal with stressors...."

   a. Related to the mind

   b. Related to biological functions

   c. Related to stress

   d. Related to medicine

4. "Still, it is typically negative events that have the most *adverse* psychological and physical effects."

   a. Minor

   b. Rapid

   c. Irreversible

   d. Harmful

5. "Daily hassles include irritations, pressures, and annoyances that might not be significant stressors by themselves but whose *cumulative* effects can be significant."

   a. Immediate

   b. Decreasing over time

   c. Increasing or enlarging by accumulation

   d. Negative

Circle the letter of the correct response.

6. Based upon Figure 13.1, which of the following is an accurate conclusion?

   a. Daily hassles are a stress response.

   b. Stress mediators affect both stressors and stress responses.

    c. Chronic stressors always produce emotional behavioral responses.

    d. If a person does not have social support, then a life change will produce cognitive stress responses.

7. Environmental circumstances that disrupt, or threaten to disrupt, individuals' daily functioning and cause people to make adjustments are called

    a. stress.

    b. stressors.

    c. stress mediators.

    d. stress responses.

8. Which of the following is NOT a kind of psychological stressor?

    a. Catastrophic events

    b. Chronic stressors

    c. Stress mediators

    d. Life changes

9. Aretha had a tough week filled with many stressful events. Which one of them was a chronic stressor?

    a. A water pipe burst and filled her office with water. Most of the files she had been working on were totally ruined.

    b. On the subway on her way to work, a person splashed Aretha's suit jacket with a can of soda he was drinking.

    c. Her daughter was diagnosed with diabetes.

    d. Another poor company quarterly report meant that she would have to do without a much-needed raise.

Chemistry: "The Scientific Method"

Actively read the excerpt from a chemistry textbook, and then answer the questions that follow.

nature. The first thing you did was collect relevant data. Then you made a prediction, and then you tested it by trying it out. This process contains the fundamental elements of science.

1. Making observations (collecting data)

2. Making a prediction (formulating a hypothesis)

3. Doing experiments to test the prediction (testing the hypothesis)

Scientists call this process the *scientific method*. We will discuss it in more detail in the next section. One of life's most important activities is solving problems—not "plug and chug" exercises, but real problems—problems that have new facets to them, that involve things you may have never confronted before. The more creative you are at solving these problems, the more effective you will be in your career and your personal life. Part of the reason for learning chemistry, therefore, is to become a better problem solver. Chemists are usually excellent problem solvers, because to master chemistry, you have to master the scientific approach. Chemical problems are frequently very complicated—there is usually no neat and tidy solution. Often it is difficult to know where to begin.

1.2   The Scientific Method

Science is a framework for gaining and organizing knowledge. Science is not simply a set of facts but also a plan of action—a *procedure* for processing and understanding certain types of information. Scientific thinking is useful in all aspects of life, but in this text we will use it to understand how the chemical world operates. As we have said in our previous discussion, the process that lies at the center of scientific inquiry is called the **scientific method.** There are actually many scientific methods, depending on the nature of the specific problem under study and on the particular investigator involved. However, it is useful to consider the following general framework for a generic scientific method (see Fig. 1.4):

Steps in the Scientific Method

➡ 1 *Making observations.* Observations may be *qualitative* (the sky is blue; water is a liquid) or *quantitative* (water boils at 100°C; a certain chemistry book weighs 2 kilograms). A qualitative observation does not involve a number. A quantitative observation (called a **measurement**) involves both a number and a unit.

➡ 2 *Formulating hypotheses.* A **hypothesis** is a *possible* explanation for an observation.

➡ 3 *Performing experiments.* An experiment is carried out to test a hypothesis. This involves gathering new information that enables a scientist to decide whether the hypothesis is valid—that is, whether it is supported by the new information learned from the experiment. Experiments always produce new observations, and this brings the process back to the beginning again.

To understand a given phenomenon, these steps are repeated many times, gradually accumulating the knowledge necessary to provide a possible explanation of the phenomenon.

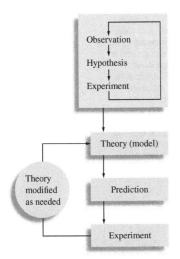

FIGURE 1.4
The fundamental steps of the scientific method.

Once a set of hypotheses that agrees with the various observations is obtained, the hypotheses are assembled into a theory. A **theory,** which is often called a **model,** is a set of tested hypotheses that gives an overall explanation of some natural phenomenon.

It is very important to distinguish between observations and theories. An observation is something that is witnessed and can be recorded. A theory is an *interpretation*—a possible explanation of *why* nature behaves in a particular way. Theories inevitably change as more information becomes available. For example, the motions of the sun and stars have remained virtually the same over the thousands of years during which humans have been observing them, but our explanations— our theories—for these motions have changed greatly since ancient times. (See the Chemical Impact on Observations, Theories, and the Planets on the Web site.

The point is that scientists do not stop asking questions just because a given theory seems to account satisfactorily for some aspect of natural behavior. They continue doing experiments to refine or replace the existing theories. This is generally done by using the currently accepted theory to make a prediction and then performing an experiment (making a new observation) to see whether the results bear out this prediction.

Always remember that theories (models) are human inventions. They represent attempts to explain observed natural behavior in terms of human experiences. A theory is actually an educated guess. We must continue to do experiments and to refine our theories (making them consistent with new knowledge) if we hope to approach a more nearly complete understanding of nature.

As scientists observe nature, they often see that the same observation applies to many different systems. For example, studies of innumerable chemical changes have shown that the total observed mass of the materials involved is the same before and after the change. Such generally observed behavior is formulated into a statement called a **natural law.** For example, the observation that the total mass of materials is not affected by a chemical change in those materials is called the **law of conservation of mass.**

Note the difference between a natural law and a theory. A natural law is a summary of observed (measurable) behavior, whereas a theory is an explanation of behavior. *A law summarizes what happens; a theory (model) is an attempt to explain why it happens.*

In this section we have described the scientific method as it might ideally be applied (see Fig. 1.5). However, it is important to remember that science does not always progress smoothly and efficiently. For one thing, hypotheses and observations are not totally independent of each other, as we have assumed in the description of the idealized scientific method. The coupling of observations and hypotheses occurs because once we begin to proceed down a given theoretical path, our hypotheses are unavoidably couched in the language of that theory. In other words, we tend to see what we expect to see and often fail to notice things that we do not expect. Thus the theory we are testing helps us because it focuses our questions. However, at the very same time, this focusing process may limit our ability to see other possible explanations.

It is also important to keep in mind that scientists are human. They have prejudices; they misinterpret data; they become emotionally attached to their theories and thus lose objectivity; and they play politics. Science is affected by profit motives, budgets, fads, wars, and religious beliefs. Galileo, for example, was forced to recant his astronomical observations in the face of strong religious resistance.

8   Chapter One   Chemical Foundations

Robert Boyle (1627–1691) was born in Ireland. He became especially interested in experiments involving air and developed an air pump with which he produced evacuated cylinders. He used these cylinders to show that a feather and a lump of lead fall at the same rate in the absence of air resistance and that sound cannot be produced in a vacuum. His most famous experiments involved careful measurements of the volume of a gas as a function of pressure. In his book *The Skeptical Chymist*, Boyle urged that the ancient view of elements as mystical substances should be abandoned and that an element should instead be defined as anything that cannot be broken down into simpler substances. This conception was an important step in the development of modern chemistry.

Lavoisier, the father of modern chemistry, was beheaded because of his political affiliations. Great progress in the chemistry of nitrogen fertilizers resulted from the desire to produce explosives to fight wars. The progress of science is often affected more by the frailties of humans and their institutions than by the limitations of scientific measuring devices. The scientific methods are only as effective as the humans using them. They do not automatically lead to progress.

1.3   Units of Measurement

Making observations is fundamental to all science. A quantitative observation, or *measurement,* always consists of two parts: a *number* and a scale (called a *unit*). Both parts must be present for the measurement to be meaningful.

In this textbook we will use measurements of mass, length, time, temperature, electric current, and the amount of a substance, among others. Scientists recognized long ago that standard systems of units had to be adopted if measurements were to be useful. If every scientist had a different set of units, complete chaos would result. Unfortunately, different standards were adopted in different parts of the world. The two major systems are the *English system* used in the United States and the *metric system* used by most of the rest of the industrialized world. This duality causes a good deal of trouble; for example, parts as simple as bolts are not interchangeable between machines built using the two systems. As a result, the United States has begun to adopt the metric system.

Soda is commonly sold in 2-liter bottles—an example of the use of SI units in everyday life.

TABLE 1.1   The Fundamental SI Units

Physical Quantity	Name of Unit	Abbreviation
Mass	kilogram	kg
Length	meter	m
Time	second	s
Temperature	kelvin	K
Electric current	ampere	A
Amount of substance	mole	mol
Luminous intensity	candela	cd

1. Write a brief definition for each of the following key terms in this section:

    a. Scientific method: _____

    b. Hypothesis: _____

    c. Theory: _____

    d. Model: _____

    e. Natural law: _____

    f. Law of conservation of mass: _____

2. How many steps are there in the scientific method?

    a. Two   c. Four

    b. Three   d. Ten

The following sentences appear in the chapter. Circle the letter of the BEST meaning for each italicized word.

3. "... it is useful to consider the following general framework for a *generic* scientific method."

    a. General, not specific   c. Brief

    b. Genuine, not fake   d. Effective

4. "... studies of *innumerable* chemical changes have shown that the total observed mass of the materials involved is the same before and after the change."

    a. Occurring instantly

    b. Significant

    c. Few

    d. Too many to be counted

5. "Galileo, for example, was forced to *recant* his astronomical observations in the face of strong religious resistance."

    a. Take back

    b. Change

    c. Prove

    d. Explain

Circle the letter of the correct response.

6. Based upon Figure 1.4 in the excerpt, which of the following conclusions is accurate?

    a. A theory is formed before a hypothesis is formed.

    b. Both a hypothesis and a theory are tested with experiments.

    c. A theory does not change, regardless of the results of an experiment.

    d. A theory is modified before an experiment is complete.

Write your answers to the following review and discussion questions on the blanks provided.

7. Summarize the steps of the scientific method.

   _____

   _____

   _____

   _____

   _____

8. Explain the difference between a law and a theory.

   _____

   _____

   _____

   _____

   _____

9. Is the scientific method suitable for solving problems only in the sciences? Explain.

   _____

   _____

   _____

   _____

   _____

10. The authors state, "The progress of science is often affected more by the frailties of humans and their institutions than by the limitations of scientific measuring devices." They illustrate this statement with the examples of Galileo, Lavoisier, and the creation of nitrogen fertilizers. Think of another example or two to illustrate this statement.

    _____

    _____

    _____

    _____

    _____

Humanities: "Impressionism"

Read the humanities excerpt, and then answer the questions that follow.

Figure 22.5   Honoré Daumier, *Third Class Carriage*, 1863–1865, 25 3/4″ × 35 1/2″ (65.4 x 90.2 cm), oil on canvas, The Metropolitan Museum of Art, New York.   The viewer is an anonymous fellow passenger in a crowded public transit carriage reserved for the poor. Rather than existing as portraits of individual people, these people represent the poor in spirit as well as the poor in possessions. *(The Metropolitan Musem of Art, H.O. Havemeyer Collection, Bequest of Mrs. H.O. Havemeyer, 1929 [29.100.129] Photograph © 1985 The Metropolitan Museum of Art)*

IMPRESSIONISM

The generation of French painters who followed the Realists is termed Impressionists. *Impressionism* was the logical extension of the Realists' preoccupation with light and color. Impressionists generally concluded that what they saw was not the object itself, but rather light reflecting from objects, forms, and surfaces. Intrigued by the impact that light has on objects, Impressionists left their studios for the countryside, where they painted landscapes or scenes of contemporary life under an open sky. The Impressionists began a major breach with the Renaissance tradition because their real subject was light rather than the scenes themselves. They attempted to understand the permutations of light and color, "to get an impression of," or to capture the moment when the eye perceives light on various surfaces during different times of the day. The Impressionists also violated the Renaissance traditions of perspective and three-dimensional space by acknowledging the two-dimensional surface of the painting. A contemporary observer explained the Impressionists' interest with painting scenes naturally:

[T]he Impressionist is . . . a modernist painter endowed with an uncommon sensibility of the eye. He is one who, forgetting the pictures amassed through the centuries in museums, forgetting his optical art school training—line, perspective, color—by dint of living and seeing frankly and primitively in the bright open air, that is, outside his poorly lighted studio, whether the city street, the country, or the interiors of houses, has succeeded in remaking for himself a natural eye, and in seeing naturally and painting as simply as he sees.[10]

Like the Realists, the Impressionists depicted ordinary experiences and everyday life. But in contrast to the Realists, whose subjects were drawn from rural toil and lower-class life, Impressionists painted the middle class at leisure.

The movement began in 1874 when several artists whose works were not in harmony with the ideals of the official Salon organized an independent exhibition of their work. One of the paintings exhibited was Claude Monet's *Impression—Sunrise*, from which the term "Impressionism" is derived. Between 1874 and 1886, the Impressionists held eight more of these independent exhibitions.

The following sentences appear in the chapter. Circle the letter of the BEST meaning for each italicized word or phrase.

1. "The Impressionists began a major *breach with* the Renaissance tradition...."

    a. Revival of   c. Break with

    b. Study of   d. Blending with

2. "They attempted to understand the *permutations* of light and color...."

    a. Mixtures   c. Sources

    b. Meanings   d. Changes

3. "... in contrast to the Realists, whose subjects were drawn from rural *toil* and lower-class life, Impressionists painted the middle class at leisure."

    a. Poverty   c. Labor

    b. Recreation   d. Towns

Write your answers to the following review and discussion questions on the blanks provided.

4. What were the basic artistic aims of Impressionism?

    _____

    _____

    _____

5. How were Impressionist artists like Realist artists? How were they different?

    _____

    _____

    _____

6. In what ways did Impressionism break with the Renaissance tradition?

    _____

    _____

    _____

7. From where did the term *Impressionism* originate?

    _____

    _____

    _____

8. Fill in the blanks in the following summary of this section of the chapter:

Impressionism emerged as a logical extension of _____. However, while

Realists focused on _____ themselves, the Impressionists attended to

the effects of _____ and _____ on surfaces, thus

breaking significantly with the _____ tradition. Further, although the

Impressionists shared the Realists' interest in _____, they generally

depicted _____ rather than _____.

9. Write a paragraph about what you learned from reading this material about Impressionism.
   Did any of the information surprise you? Did it contradict any of your previous knowledge
   about the topic?

_____

_____

_____

_____

_____

_____

_____

_____

_____

_____

Long Textbook Excerpts

*Now that you have practiced with short textbook excerpts, apply your reading skills to two longer chapter
excerpts. One is from a Physical Science textbook and the other from a Business textbook.*

An Introduction to Physical Science: "Atmospheric Effects"

Preview the chapter entitled "Atmospheric Effects," and then answer the following questions.

1. On what topics does this chapter focus?

   a. Rain and storms

   b. Weather, climate, and pollution

   c. Keeping the environment clean

   d. The planet Earth

2. Into how many major sections is this chapter divided?

    a. Two   c. Live

    b. Three   d. Eight

3. Where are the learning goals of this chapter located?

    a. In a list at the beginning of the chapter

    b. In a list at the end of the chapter

    c. In the margins throughout the chapter

    d. Within the text of the chapter

4. True or False: In this chapter, key terms are defined in the margins.

    a. True   b. False

5. Which of the following is NOT an action you should be able to perform after reading this chapter?

    a. Distinguish among the various types of precipitation.

    b. Identify various types of local and tropical storms.

    c. Define *climate* and identify climatic changes.

    d. Identify the major types of water pollution.

6. Locate the list of key terms in the chapter. In this chapter, they are known as

    a. key terms.   c. important terms.

    b. vocabulary.   d. words to know.

7. Based on the chapter outline, you can reasonably conclude that this chapter will NOT cover

    a. tornadoes.

    b. smog.

    c. how the moon affects ocean tides.

    d. sources of air pollution.

8. Into what two major categories does the author divide storms?

    a. Local storms and tropical storms

    b. Thunder and lightning

    c. Tornadoes and hurricanes

    d. Thunderstorms and tropical storms

Before you read the excerpt, turn all of the headings and subheadings into questions. Then highlight or underline the answers to those questions. If you encounter an unfamiliar word, look it up in a dictionary and write its definition in the margin.

Atmospheric Effects

And pleas'd the Almighty's orders to perform

Rides in the whirlwind and directs the storm.

Joseph Addison (1672–1719)

Photo: Lightning—a most
spectacular atmospheric effect.

It is not just farmers who are concerned with the daily and future weather conditions. Readily available weather reports and forecasts help us decide such things as how we should dress for the day, whether to take an umbrella along, and whether a weekend picnic should be canceled. The weather changes frequently, because the lower atmosphere is a very dynamic place.

The air we now breathe may have been far out over the Pacific Ocean a week ago. As air moves into a region, it brings with it the temperature and humidity of previous locations. Cold, dry, arctic air may cause a sudden drop in the temperature of the regions in its path. Warm, moist air from the Gulf of Mexico may bring heat and humidity and make the summer seem unbearable.

Thus moving air transports the physical characteristics that influence the weather and produce changes. A large mass of air can influence the region for a considerable period of time, or it can have only a brief effect. The movement of air masses depends heavily on the Earth's air circulation structure and seasonal variations.

When air masses meet, variations of their properties may trigger storms along their common boundary. Thus the types of storms depend on the properties of the air masses involved. Also, variations within a single air mass can give rise to storms locally. Storms can be violent and sometimes destructive. They remind us of the vast amount of

522

energy contained in the atmosphere and also of its capability. As we shall see in this chapter, the variations of our weather are closely associated with air masses and their movements and interactions.

An unfortunate issue in atmospheric science is pollution. Various pollutants are being released into the atmosphere, thereby affecting our health, living conditions, and environment.

Climate also may be affected by pollution. For example, we hear about *acid rain*. Government restrictions have helped reduce this problem, but what about the "ozone hole" and CFCs? These topics will be considered in this chapter. ■

20.1 Condensation and Precipitation

LEARNING GOALS

▼ Explain how precipitation is formed.

▼ Distinguish among the various types of precipitation.

In the preceding chapter's section on cloud formation, we noted that condensation occurs in an air mass when the dew point is reached. However, it is quite possible for an air mass containing water vapor to be cooled below the dew point without condensation occurring. In this state, the air mass is said to be *supersaturated*, or *supercooled*.

How, then, are visible droplets of water formed? You might think that the collision and coalescing of water molecules would form a droplet. But this event would require the collision of millions of molecules. Moreover, only after a small droplet has reached a critical size will it have sufficient binding force to retain additional molecules. The probability of a droplet forming by this process is quite remote.

Instead, water droplets form around microscopic foreign particles called *hygroscopic nuclei* that are already present in the air. These particles are in the form of dust, combustion residue (smoke and soot), salt from seawater evaporation, and so forth. Because foreign particles initiate the formation of droplets that eventually fall as precipitation, condensation provides a mechanism for cleansing the atmosphere.

Liquid water may be cooled below the freezing point (supercooled) without the formation of ice if it does not contain the proper type of foreign particles

to act as ice nuclei. For many years scientists believed that ice nuclei could be just about anything, such as dust. However, research has shown that "clean" dust—that is, dust without biological materials from plants or bacteria—will not act as ice nuclei. This discovery is important because precipitation involves ice crystals, as will be discussed shortly.

Because cooling and condensation occur in updrafts, the formed droplets are readily suspended in the air as a cloud. For precipitation, larger droplets or drops must form. This condition may be brought about by two processes: (1) coalescence and/or (2) the Bergeron process.

Coalescence

Coalescence is the formation of drops by the collision of droplets, the result being that larger droplets grow at the expense of smaller ones. The efficiency of this process depends on the variation in the size of the droplets.

Raindrops vary in size, reaching a maximum diameter of approximately 7 mm. A drop 1 mm in diameter would require the coalescing of a million droplets of 10-μm (micrometer) diameter but only 1000 droplets of 100-μm diameter. Thus we see that having larger droplets greatly enhances the coalescence process.

Bergeron Process

The **Bergeron process**, named after the Swedish meteorologist who suggested it, is probably the more important process for the initiation of precipitation. This process involves clouds that contain ice crystals in their upper portions and have become supercooled in their lower portions (● Fig. 20.1).

Mixing or agitation within such a cloud allows the ice crystals to come into contact with the supercooled vapor. Acting as nuclei, the ice crystals grow larger from the vapor condensing on them. The ice crystals melt into large droplets in the warmer, lower portion of the cloud and coalesce to fall as precipitation. Air currents are the normal mixing agents.

Note that there are three essentials in the Bergeron process: (1) ice crystals, (2) supercooled vapor, and (3) mixing. *Rainmaking* is based on the essentials of the Bergeron process.

The early rainmakers were mostly charlatans. With much ceremony, they would beat on drums or fire

524   **Chapter 20   ATMOSPHERIC EFFECTS**

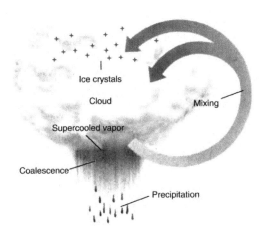

FIGURE 20.1   The Bergeron Process
The essence of the Bergeron process is the mixing of ice crystals and supercooled vapor, which produces water droplets and initiates precipitation.

cannons and rockets into the air. Explosives may have supplied the agitation or mixing for rainmaking, assuming that the other two essentials of the Bergeron process were present.

However, modern rainmakers use a different approach. There are usually enough air currents present for mixing, but the ice crystal nuclei may be lacking. To correct this, they "seed" clouds with silver iodide crystals or dry-ice pellets (solid CO_2).

The silver iodide crystals have a structure similar to that of ice and provide a substitute for ice crystals. Silver iodide crystals are produced by a burning process. The burning may be done on the ground, with the iodide crystals being carried aloft by the rising warm air, or the burner may be attached to an airplane and the process carried out in a cloud to be seeded.

Dry-ice pellets are seeded into a cloud from an airplane. The pellets do not act as nuclei but serve another purpose. The temperature of solid dry ice is −79°C (−110°F), and it quickly sublimes—that is, goes directly from the solid to the gaseous phase. Rapid cooling associated with the sublimation triggers the conversion of supercooled cloud droplets into ice crystals. Precipitation may then occur if this part of the Bergeron process has been absent.

Also, the latent heat released from the ice crystal formation is available to set up convection cycles for

mixing. Seeding may also come to be widely used for initiating the precipitation of fog, which frequently hinders airport operations.

Types of Precipitation

Precipitation can occur in the form of rain, snow, sleet, hail, dew, or fog depending on atmospheric conditions. *Rain* is the most common form of precipitation in the lower and middle latitudes. The formation of large water drops that fall as rain has been described previously.

If the dew point is below 0°C, the water vapor freezes on condensing, and the ice crystals that result fall as *snow*. In cold regions, these ice crystals may fall individually. In warmer regions, the ice crystals become stuck together, forming a snowflake that may be as much as 2 to 3 cm across. Because ice crystallizes in a hexagonal (six-sided) pattern, snowflakes are hexagonal (see Fig. 2 on page 96).

Frozen rain, or pellets of ice in the form of *sleet*, occurs when rain falls through a cold surface layer of air and freezes or, more often, when the ice pellets fall directly from the cloud without melting before striking the ground. Large pellets of ice, or *hail*, result from successive vertical descents and ascents in vigorous convection cycles associated with thunderstorms. Additional condensation on successive cycles into supercooled regions that are below freezing may produce layered-structure hailstones the size of golf balls and baseballs. When hailstones are cut in two, the layers of ice can be observed, much like the rings in tree growth (● Fig. 20.2).

Dew is formed by atmospheric water vapor condensing on various surfaces. The land cools quickly at night, particularly with no cloud cover, and the temperature may fall below the dew point. Water vapor then condenses on available surfaces such as blades of grass, giving rise to the "early morning dew."

If the dew point is below freezing, the water vapor condenses in the form of ice crystals as *frost*. Frost is *not* frozen dew but, rather, results from the direct change of water vapor into ice (the reverse of sublimation, called *deposition*).

Interestingly, research has shown that frost is a result of bacteria-seeded ice formation. Without two common types of bacteria on leaf surfaces, water will not freeze at 0°C but can be supercooled to −6° to −8°C. These bacteria exist on plants, fruit trees, and so on and serve as nuclei for frost formation.

FIGURE 20.2 Hailstones
The successive vertical ascents of ice pellets into supercooled air and regions of condensation produce large, layered "stones" of ice. The layered structure can be seen in these cross sections.

With frost damage to crops and fruits exceeding $1 billion annually, scientists are exploring techniques to prevent the formation of bacteria-seeded frost. One method involves the development of genetically engineered bacteria, which are altered such that they can no longer trigger ice formation.

Researchers believe that a protein on the surface of the bacterium acts as the seed for the formation of frost ice crystals. They hope that "frost-free" bacteria can be made by genetically removing the gene that serves as the blueprint for this protein.

RELEVANCE QUESTION: *By late morning or early afternoon the morning dew you observe is gone. Where does it go?*

20.2 Air Masses

LEARNING GOALS

▼ Define *air masses*, and tell how they are classified.

▼ Identify fronts and their effects on local weather.

As we know, the weather changes with time. However, we often experience several days of relatively uniform weather conditions. Our general weather conditions depend in large part on vast air masses that move across the country.

When a large body of air takes on physical characteristics that distinguish it from the surrounding air, it is referred to as an **air mass**. The main distinguishing characteristics are *temperature* and *moisture content*.

A mass of air remaining for some time over a particular region, such as a large body of land or water, takes on the physical characteristics of the surface of the region. The region from which an air mass derives its characteristics is called its **source region**.

An air mass eventually moves from its source region, bringing its characteristics to regions in its path and thus bringing changes in the weather. As an air mass travels, its properties may become modified because of local variations. For example, if Canadian polar air masses did not become warmer as they travel southward, Florida would experience some extremely cold temperatures.

Whether an air mass is termed *cold* or *warm* is relative to the surface over which it moves. Quite logically, if an air mass is warmer than the land surface, it is referred to as a *warm air mass*. If the air is colder than the surface, it is called a *cold air mass*. Remember, though, that these terms are relative. *Warm* and *cold* do not always imply warm and cold weather. A "warm" air mass in winter may not raise the temperature above freezing.

Air masses are classified according to the surface and general latitude of their source regions:

Surface	*Latitude*
Maritime (m)	Arctic (A)
Continental (c)	Polar (P)
	Tropical (T)
	Equatorial (E)

The surface of the source region, abbreviated by a small letter, gives an indication of the moisture content of an air mass. An air mass forming over a body of water (maritime) would naturally be expected to have a greater moisture content than one forming over land (continental).

The general latitude of a source region, abbreviated by a capital letter, gives an indication of the temperature of an air mass. For example, "mT" designates a maritime tropical air mass, which would be expected to be a warm, moist one. The air masses that affect the weather in the United States are listed in Table 20.1, along with their source regions, and are illustrated in ● Fig. 20.3.

The movement of air masses is influenced to a great extent by the Earth's general circulation patterns

526   Chapter 20   ATMOSPHERIC EFFECTS

TABLE 20.1 Air Masses That Affect the Weather of the United States

Classification	Symbol	Source Region
Maritime arctic	mA	Arctic regions
Continental arctic	cA	Greenland
Maritime polar	mP	Northern Atlantic and Pacific oceans
Continental polar	cP	Alaska and Canada
Maritime tropical	mT	Caribbean Sea, Gulf of Mexico, and Pacific Ocean
Continental tropical	cT	Northern Mexico, southwestern United States

(Section 19.4). Because the conterminous United States lies predominantly in the westerlies zone, the general movement of air masses—and hence of the weather—is from west to east across the country. Global circulation zones vary to some extent in latitude with the seasons, and the polar easterlies may also move air masses into the eastern United States during the winter.

The boundary between two air masses is called a **front**. A *warm front* is the boundary of an advancing warm air mass over a colder surface, and a *cold front* is the boundary of a cold air mass moving over a warmer surface. These boundaries, called *frontal zones*, may vary in width from a few miles to over 160 km (100 mi). It is along fronts, which divide air masses of different physical characteristics, that drastic changes in weather occur. Turbulent weather and storms usually characterize a front.

The degree and rate of weather change depend on the difference in temperature of the air masses and on the degree of vertical slope of a front. A cold front moving into a warmer region causes the lighter,

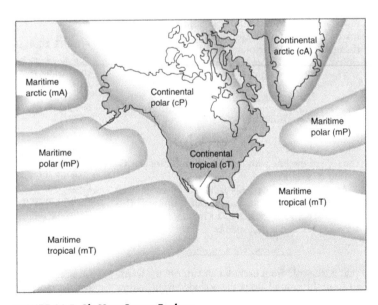

FIGURE 20.3 Air-Mass Source Regions
The map shows the source regions for the air masses of North America.

warm air to be displaced upward over the front (● Fig. 20.4). The lighter air of the advancing warm front cannot displace the heavier, colder air as readily, and generally it moves slowly up and over the colder air.

Heavier, colder air is associated with high pressure, and this downward divergent air flow in a high-pressure region generally gives a cold front greater speed than a warm front. A cold front may have an average speed of 30 to 40 km/h (20 to 25 mi/h), whereas a warm front averages about 15 to 25 km/h (10 to 15 mi/h).

Cold fronts have sharper vertical boundaries than warm fronts, and warm air is displaced upward faster by an advancing cold front. As a result, cold fronts are accompanied by more violent or sudden changes in weather. The sudden decrease in temperature is often described as a "cold snap." Dark altocumulus clouds often mark a cold front's approach (Fig. 20.4). The sudden cooling and the rising warm air may set off rainstorm or snowstorm activity along the front.

A warm front also may be characterized by precipitation and storms. Because the approach of a warm front is more gradual, it is usually heralded by a period of lowering clouds. Cirrus and mackerel scale (cirrocumulus) clouds drift ahead of the front, followed by alto clouds. As the front approaches, cumulus or cumulonimbus clouds that result from the rising air produce precipitation and storms. Most precipitation occurs before the front passes.

The graphical symbol for a cold front is

and for a warm front is

The side of the line with the symbol indicates the direction of advance.

As a faster-moving cold front advances, it may overtake a warm air mass and push it upward. The boundary between these two air masses is called an *occluded front* and is indicated by

That is, the cold front occludes, or cuts off, the warm air from the ground along the occluded front. When a cold front advances under a warm front, a *cold front occlusion* results. When a warm front advances up and over a cold front, the air ahead is colder than the

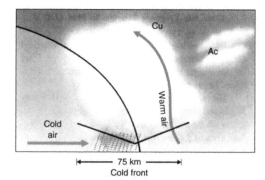

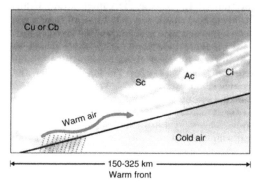

FIGURE 20.4 Side Views of Cold and Warm Fronts
Note in the upper diagram the sharp, steep boundary that is characteristic of cold fronts. The boundary of a warm front, as shown in the lower diagram, is less steep. As a result, different cloud types are associated with the approach of the two types of fronts. (See the table on page 517 for cloud abbreviations.)

advancing air, and the occluded front is referred to as a *warm front occlusion.*

Sometimes fronts traveling in opposite directions meet. The opposing fronts may balance each other so that no movement occurs. This case is referred to as a *stationary front* and is indicated by

Air masses and fronts move across the country bringing changes in weather. Dynamic situations give rise to cyclonic disturbances around low-pressure and high-pressure regions. As we saw in Chapter 19, these disturbances are called *cyclones* and *anticyclones*, respectively (see Fig. 19.20).

528 Chapter 20 ATMOSPHERIC EFFECTS

As a low or cyclone moves, it carries with it rising air currents, clouds, possibly precipitation, and generally bad weather. Hence lows or cyclones are usually associated with poor weather, whereas highs or anticyclones are usually associated with good weather. The lack of rising air and cloud formation in highs gives clear skies and fair weather. Because of their influence on the weather, the movements of highs and lows are closely monitored.

We usually think of a source region as being relatively hot or cold. But significant variations can occur within a source region at a particular latitude, giving rise to abnormal weather conditions. A classic example, El Niño, is discussed in the chapter's first Highlight on page 530.

RELEVANCE QUESTION: Which types of air masses (see Table 20.1) generally affect your weather?

20.3 Storms

LEARNING GOALS

▼ Identify various types of local and tropical storms.

▼ Describe the aspects of lightning safety and tornado safety.

Storms are atmospheric disturbances that may develop locally within a single air mass or may be due to frontal activity along the boundary of air masses. Several types of storms, distinguished by their intensity and violence, will be considered. These will be divided generally into local storms and tropical storms.

Local Storms

There are several types of local storms. A heavy downpour is commonly referred to as a *rainstorm*. Storms with rainfalls of 1 to 3 inches per hour are not uncommon.

A *thunderstorm* is a rainstorm distinguished by thunder and lightning, and sometimes hail. The **lightning** associated with a thunderstorm is a discharge of electrical energy. In the turmoil of a thundercloud or "thunderhead," there is a separation of charge associated with the breaking up and movement of water droplets. This gives rise to an electric potential. When this is of sufficient magnitude, lightning occurs.

FIGURE 20.5 Lightning
Lightning discharges can occur between a cloud and the Earth, between clouds, and within a cloud.

Lightning can take place entirely within a cloud (intracloud or cloud discharges), between two clouds (cloud-to-cloud discharges), between a cloud and the Earth (cloud-to-ground or ground discharges), or between a cloud and the surrounding air (air discharges). See ● Fig. 20.5.

Lightning has reportedly even occurred in clear air, apparently giving rise to the expression "a bolt from the blue." When lightning occurs below the horizon or behind clouds, it often illuminates the clouds with flickering flashes. This commonly occurs on a still summer night and is known as *heat lightning*.

Although the most frequently occurring form of lightning is the intracloud discharge, of greatest concern is lightning between a cloud and the Earth. The shorter the distance from a cloud to the ground, the more easily the electric discharge takes place. For this reason, lightning often strikes trees and tall buildings. It is inadvisable, therefore, to take shelter from a thunderstorm under a tree. A person in the vicinity of a lightning strike may experience an electric shock that causes breathing to fail. In such a case, mouth-to-mouth resuscitation or some other form of artificial respiration should be given immediately, and the person should be kept warm as a treatment for shock. (See the following discussion of lightning safety.)

The following sentences appear in the chapter. Circle the letter of the BEST meaning for each italicized word.

9. "You might think that the collision and *coalescing* of water molecules would form a droplet."

   a. Striking

   b. Evaporating

   c. Separating

   d. Uniting

10. "The *probability* of a droplet forming by this process is quite remote."

    a. Percentage

    b. Likelihood

    c. Certainty

    d. Occurrence

    "The probability of a droplet forming by this process is quite *remote*."

    a. Far

    b. Near

    c. Slight

    d. Possible

11. "Mixing or *agitation* within such a cloud allows the ice crystals to come into contact with the supercooled vapor.

    a. Violent movement

    b. Expansion

    c. Floating

    d. Hostile behavior

12. "The early rainmakers were mostly *charlatans*."

    a. Frauds

    b. Powerful magicians

    c. Generous people

    d. Leaders

13. "*Turbulent* weather and storms usually characterize a front."

    a. Swollen

    b. Violently disturbed

    c. Fast-moving

    d. Very cold

Circle the letter of the correct response.

14. Based on Table 20.1 in the preceding section of the physical science chapter, which of the following conclusions is accurate?

a. The continental arctic air mass affects the weather of the United States more than the other air masses.

b. The continental polar air mass originates in Alaska and Canada.

c. The maritime tropical air mass originates in Mexico.

d. The Pacific Ocean is the source of only the maritime polar air mass.

15. Based on Figure 20.1 in the preceding section of the physical science chapter, you can conclude that

a. ice crystals are in the upper portion of a cloud.

b. the ice crystals freeze to form precipitation.

c. the lower portion of the cloud is colder than the upper portion.

d. supercooled vapor is outside the cloud.

16. When the temperature of the air is below the dew point without precipitation, the air is said to be what?

a. Stable

b. Supercooled

c. Sublimed

d. Coalesced

17. Which of the following is NOT essential to the Bergeron process?

a. Silver iodide

b. Mixing

c. Supercooled vapor

d. Ice crystals

18. Describe the three essentials of the Bergeron process and how they are related to methods of modern rainmaking.

_____

_____

_____

19. Is frost frozen dew? Explain. How are large hailstones formed?

_____

_____

_____

20. Which of the following air masses would be expected to be cold and dry?

    a. cP   c. cT

    b. mA   d. mE

21. A cold front advancing under a warm front is called a

    a. warm front.   c. cold front occlusion.

    b. stationary front.   d. warm front occlusion.

22. How are air masses classified? Explain the relationship between air-mass characteristics and source regions.

    _____

    _____

    _____

23. Give the source region(s) of the air mass(es) that affect the weather in your area.

    _____

    _____

    _____

24. What is a front? List the meteorological symbols for four types of fronts.

    _____

    _____

    _____

25. Describe the weather associated with warm fronts and with cold fronts. What is the significance of the sharpness of their vertical boundaries?

    _____

    _____

    _____

Discuss the following questions with a partner or group, and then collaborate to write a response to each question on your own paper.

26. By late morning or early afternoon, the morning dew you observe is gone. Where does it go?

    _____

    _____

    _____

27.   Which types of air masses (see Table 20.1 in the preceding section of the physical science chapter) generally affect your weather?

_____

_____

_____

_____

_____

_____

_____

_____

Business: "Exploring the World of Business"

Preview the chapter, and then answer the questions that follow.

1.   How many learning objectives are there for this chapter?

   a. One

   b. Three

   c. Five

   d. Seven

2.   Which of the following is NOT something you should be able to do when you have finished reading the chapter?

   a. Describe two types of economic systems.

   b. Outline four types of competition.

   c. Explain how to be successful in international business.

   d. Discuss future challenges for American business.

3.   True or False: This chapter provides definitions of key terms.

   a. True

   b. False

Before you read the excerpt, turn all of the headings into questions. Then read actively by either highlighting or underlining the answers to those questions. If you encounter an unfamiliar word, look it up in a dictionary and write its definition in the margin.

1

exploring the world of business

This year, General Electric was chosen as America's most admired corporation for the third year in a row.

LEARNING OBJECTIVES

1 Discuss your future in the world of business.

2 Define *business* and identify potential risks and rewards.

3 Describe the two types of economic systems: capitalism and command economy.

4 Identify the ways to measure economic performance.

5 Outline the four types of competition.

6 Summarize the development of America's business system.

7 Discuss the challenges that American businesses will encounter in the future.

2

inside Business

3

General Electric: America's Most Admired Company

EACH YEAR FOR THE last eighteen years, *Fortune* magazine has created a list of America's most admired companies. The process begins by identifying the companies that have the highest sales revenue. This year 1,025 U.S. companies and U.S. subsidiaries of foreign-held enterprises were placed on the *Fortune* list. Corporate executives then vote on the top companies in their respective industries to help *Fortune* create a "most admired" list for practically every industry—entertainment, trucking, and medical products, to name a few. Eight specific criteria that include innovation, quality of management, employee talent, financial soundness, use of corporate assets, long-term investment value, social responsibility, and quality of products and services are used to help determine the best of the best. Then the list of top ten companies is chosen by securities analysts, corporate board members, and executives. This year, General Electric was chosen as America's Most Admired Corporation. What makes this year's award even more important is that this year is the fourth year in a row that General Electric has won this coveted award.

By now, you may be asking yourself: How could a company that makes light bulbs win this prestigious award? Although most of us know General Electric, or simply GE, as a manufacturer of light bulbs, the company is also a corporate giant consisting of over twenty different core businesses. It all started back in 1878 when Thomas Edison founded the Electric Light Company. A merger with the Thomson-Houston Electric Company before the turn of the century created the General Electric Corporation—the name we know today. This new company invented and manufactured electrical devices that ranged from the small filaments that are still used in light bulbs to the first steam turbine generator powerful enough to supply electricity to an entire city. Since then GE has expanded into many other areas of business

that range from broadcasting to financial services to silicone manufacturing. The company even built the first nuclear power plant.

While General Electric is admired by many business executives and enjoys tremendous financial success, America's most admired company is not one to sit back and rest on past performance. A program of lofty standards, called *growth initiatives,* is used to examine every facet of production and service. One growth initiative, called the *Sixth Sigma,* is a rigid process of defining, measuring, analyzing, improving, and controlling quality. Because of the Sixth Sigma, managers and employees are empowered to improve on every product the company sells, from jet engines to medical equipment.

Another growth initiative states GE's firm resolution to become the global leader in each of its core business areas. Although lesser companies often want to just sell their products or services around the world, GE doesn't just stop with selling its products or services. This award-winning company also helps the people in other nations develop their resources including raw materials and "intellectual capital." For example, GE employs over thirty thousand people and has made large investments in building manufacturing plants in Mexico. America's Most Admired Corporation is also urging its suppliers to build facilities in Mexico. And GE's global commitment doesn't stop with Mexico. Currently, the firm employs over 340,000 employees in 100 different countries around the globe.

So what if the company wins an award and is recognized as a global leader? Has time and money been invested well? Consider the following facts. The company has paid quarterly dividends to stockholders every year since 1899. One share of General Electric purchased before 1926 is now worth $245,760. Maybe, what's more important is the fact that General Electric is the "darling" of Wall Street. Financial analysts continue to recommend the stock as a "best bet" for the future.[1]

4

In today's competitive business environment, it's common to hear of profitable companies. It is less common to hear of profitable companies that are held in high regard by their competitors. That's what is so astonishing about General Electric being chosen by *Fortune* magazine as America's Most Admired Corporation for four years in a row. What's even more astonishing is that General Electric doesn't just concentrate on earning profits. The company is committed to giving back resources to the communities in which it operates. Its public service program, Elfun, consists of more than 40,000 GE employees and retirees who have just donated an annual record of 1.3 million volunteer hours working for community service projects such as food and renovation programs for the poor and also supporting mentoring programs at schools to help students and teachers in science, engineering, and math. In reality, General Electric is an excellent example of what American business should be doing.

Perhaps the most important characteristic of our economic system is the freedom of individuals to start a business, to work for a business, and to buy or sell ownership shares in the business. While business always entails risks, it can also have its rewards. For Michael Dell, the chairman, CEO, and founder of Dell Computer Corporation, there has been the satisfaction of succeeding in a very competitive industry—not to mention some very substantial financial rewards.

free enterprise the system of business in which individuals are free to decide what to produce, how to produce it, and at what price to sell it

Within certain limits, imposed mainly to ensure public safety, the owners of a business can produce any legal good or service they choose and attempt to sell it at the price they set. This system of business, in which individuals decide what to produce, how to produce it, and at what price to sell it, is called **free enterprise.** Our free-enterprise system ensures, for example, that Dell Computer can buy parts from Intel, software from Lotus Development Corporation, and manufacture its own computers. Our system gives Dell's owners and stockholders the right to make a profit from the company's success; it gives Dell's management the right to compete with Compaq and IBM; and it gives computer buyers the right to choose.

In this chapter, we look briefly at what business is and how it got that way. First, we discuss your future in business and explore some important reasons for studying business. Then we define *business,* noting how business organizations satisfy needs and earn profits. Next we examine how capitalism and command economies answer four basic economic questions. Then our focus shifts to how the nations of the world measure economic performance and the four types of competitive situations. Next we go back into American history for a look at the events that helped shape today's business system. We conclude this chapter with a discussion of the challenges that businesses face.

Your Future in the World of Business

What do you want?
Why do you want it?
Write it down!

During a segment on the Oprah Winfrey television show, Joe Dudley, one of the world's most successful Black business owners, gave the above advice to anyone who wants to succeed in business. And his advice is an excellent way to begin our discussion of what free enterprise is all about. What's so amazing about Dudley's success is that he grew up in a rural farmhouse with no running water and began his career selling Fuller Brush products door-to-door. He went on to develop his own line of hair-care products and open a chain of beauty schools and beauty supply stores. Today, Dudley is president of Dudley Products, Inc.—one of the largest minority-owned companies in the nation. Not only a successful business owner, he is the winner of the Horatio Alger Award—an award given to outstanding individuals who have succeeded in the face of adversity.[2]

Opportunity! It's only eleven letters, but no other word provides a better description of the current business environment. While many people would say that Joe Dudley was just lucky or happened to be in the right place at the right time, the truth

5

is that he became a success because he had a dream and worked hard to turn his dream into a reality. He would be the first to tell you that you have the same opportunities that he had. In fact, employment opportunities for entry-level workers, investment opportunities, and career advancement opportunities have never been greater. However, people who are successful must adapt to changes in their environment. Consider just some of the changes that have occurred since the previous edition of *Business* was published.

All work and no play? Not for this entrepreneur. Jeff Bonforte, founder and CEO of idrive.com, knows that starting a high-tech company is hard work and requires long hours, but that it can be a lot of fun. It can also be very rewarding. Bonforte is now worth an estimated $5 to $10 million.

■ Today the economy is healthy and we have experienced the longest period of sustained economic growth in our history.
■ There is a large increase in the number of new, start-up companies especially in the technology and information industries.
■ The increased use of the Internet has created new jobs that did not exist even three years ago.
■ Unemployment numbers are at record lows and employers are now recruiting new employees.
■ An increasing number of people work at home for all or part of the work week.

For the person that has the required abilities and skills, it is an excellent time to start a career. And yet, employers and our capitalistic economic system are more demanding than ever before. Ask yourself: What can I do that will make employers want to pay me a salary? What skills do I have that employers need? With these two questions in mind, we begin the next section with another basic question: Why Study Business?

Why Study Business?

Education is a unique purchase—one of the few things you can buy that will last your lifetime. It can't rust, corrode, break down, or wear out. Education can't be stolen, burned, repossessed, or destroyed. Education is a purchase that becomes a permanent part of you. Once you have it, no one can take it away.[3]

In this section, we explore what you may expect to get out of this business course and text. You will find at least four quite compelling reasons for studying business.

To Become a Better-Informed Consumer and Investor

The world of business surrounds us. You cannot buy a home, a new Trans Am from the local Pontiac dealer, a Black & Decker sander at the Home Depot, a pair of jeans at the Gap, or a hot dog from a street vendor without entering a business transaction. These and thousands of similar transactions describe the true nature of the American business system.

Using the Internet

Your Internet connection to more business information begins at **College Division** web site. Enter the web site URL **www.cengage.com/college.** Select the student tab and then go to "Business." Select the text web site or the resource center to find quick access to business journals and web sites that explore many topics discussed in the text chapters and more. This site will simplify your search for information on the Internet. Use it often to keep up to date with current developments in the fast-paced world

6

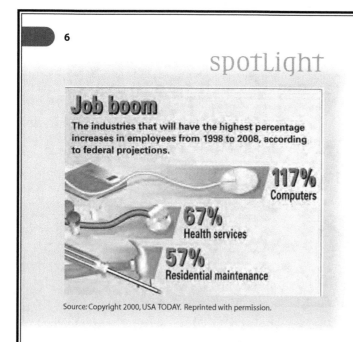

spotLight

Job boom

The industries that will have the highest percentage increases in employees from 1998 to 2008, according to federal projections.

117% Computers

67% Health services

57% Residential maintenance

Because you will no doubt engage in business transactions almost every day of your life, one very good reason for studying business is to become a more fully informed consumer. Your knowledge of business will enable you to make intelligent buying decisions and to spend your money more wisely. This same basic understanding of business will also make you a better-informed investor.

For Help in Choosing a Career What do you want to do with the rest of your life? Someplace, sometime, someone has probably asked you that same question. And like many people, you may find it a difficult question to answer. This business course will introduce you to a wide array of employment opportunities. In private enterprise, these range from small, local businesses owned by one individual to large companies like American Express and Marriott International that are owned by thousands of stockholders. There are also employment opportunities with federal, state, county, and local governments and with not-for-profit organizations like the Red Cross and Save the Children. For help deciding what career might be right for you, read Appendix A: Careers in Business. Also, you might want to read information about researching a career and the steps necessary to perform a job search that are posted on the web site that accompanies this edition of *Business*. To view this information:

1. Make an Internet connection and go to www.cengage.com/college/business
2. Locate the Student Center site and click to enter.
3. Then scroll down on the Student Center page and click on *career section.*

One thing to remember as you think about what your ideal career might be is that a person's choice of a career is ultimately just a reflection of what he or she values and holds most important. Because people have different values, they choose different careers; what will give one individual personal satisfaction may not satisfy another. For example, one person may dream of becoming a millionaire before the age of thirty. Another may choose a career that has more modest monetary rewards but that provides the opportunity to help others. One person may be willing to work long hours and seek additional responsibility in order to get promotions and pay raises. Someone else may prefer a less demanding job with little stress and more free time. What you choose to do with your life will be based on what you feel is most important.

To Be a Successful Employee Deciding on the type of career you want is only a first step. To get a job in your chosen field and to be successful at it, you will have to develop a plan, or road map, that ensures that you have the skills and knowledge the job requires. Today's employers are looking for job applicants who can *do something*, not just fill a spot on an organizational chart. You will be expected to have both the technical skills needed to accomplish a specific task and the ability to work well with many types of people in a culturally diverse work force. These skills, together with a working knowledge of the American business system, can give you an inside edge when you are interviewing with a prospective employer.

This course, your instructor, and all the resources available at your college or university can help you acquire the skills and knowledge you will need for a successful career. But don't underestimate your part in making your dream a reality. It will take hard work, dedication, perseverance, and time management to achieve your goals. Time management is especially important because it will help you accomplish the tasks that you

7

consider most important. As an added bonus, it is also a skill that employers value. Communication skills are also important. Today, most employers are looking for employees who can compose a business letter and get it in mailable form. They also want employees who can talk with customers and use e-mail to communicate to people within and outside of the organization. Employers will also be interested in any work experience you may have had in cooperative work/school programs, during summer vacations, or in part-time jobs during the school year. These things can make a difference when it is time to apply for the job you really want.

Home or office? Today more and more successful employees—like Carla Patterson, a field representative for Nebraska's Department of Economic Development—are working at home.

To Start Your Own Business   Some people prefer to work for themselves, and they open their own businesses. To be successful, business owners must possess many of the same skills that successful employees have. And they must be willing to work hard and put in long hours.

It also helps if your small business can provide a product or service that customers want. For example, Mark Cuban started a small Internet company called Broadcast.com that now provides hundreds of live and on-demand audio and video programs ranging from rap music to sporting events to business events over the Internet. This new, high-tech startup company quickly became a major player in electronic business or what many refer to as e-business. **E-business** is the organized effort of individuals to produce and sell, for a profit, the products and services that satisfy society's needs *through the facilities available on the Internet*. When Cuban sold Broadcast.com to Yahoo! Inc., he became a billionaire. Today he is an expert on how the Internet and e-business will affect society in the future and believes that many small technology firms will fail over the next ten years. According to Cuban, there is a real need for all companies—not just technology companies—to provide something that their customers want. If they don't do that, their company could very well fail.[4] For more information on how two very successful firms use e-business, read the Adapting to Change boxed feature.

e-business the organized effort of individuals to produce and sell, for a profit, the products and services that satisfy society's needs through the facilities available on the Internet

Unfortunately, many small-business firms fail; 70 percent of them fail within the first five years. The material in Chapter 6 and selected topics and examples throughout this text will help you decide whether you want to open your own business. Before proceeding to the next section, take a few minutes to familiarize yourself with the text by reading the material below.

Special Note to Students

It's important to begin reading this text with one thing in mind: *this business course doesn't have to be difficult.* In fact, we've done everything possible to eliminate the problems that students encounter in a typical class. All the features in each chapter have been evaluated and recommended by instructors with years of teaching experience. In addition, business students were asked to critique each chapter component. Based on this feedback, the text includes the following features:

8

adapting to change

E-Business Is Here to Stay

ALL ACROSS THE GLOBE, E-BUSINESS IS changing the way in which companies process purchasing orders, ship merchandise, and handle customer requests. And for companies that use e-business to increase productivity and sales, profits also increase. While doing business electronically used to be reserved for only high-tech companies, over the last few years it has become apparent that those companies that refuse to join the e-business revolution will be left behind. Consider how e-business is changing the way that Charles Schwab and Wal-Mart do business.

Charles Schwab Discount Brokerage

Today, Charles Schwab is recognized as one of the most successful discount firms in the brokerage business. The reason for this success is based on two concepts: customer service and the use of technology. Technology enables investors to not only trade online but also to research potential investments online. Back in 1975, when Schwab opened his first office, employees were taught that customer service was a top priority. To help ensure that employees were willing to help the firm's customers get top quality service, his employees were paid salaries, not commissions–a practice unheard of in the brokerage business. As a result, employees were able to spend more time with customers helping them learn how to make investment decisions. When the technology became available, it was possible for the company to extend this same philosophy to investors who wanted to trade online. Today, both stock market rookies and experienced investors use the Schwab system to trade stocks online at reduced commissions. More importantly, these same investors use research tools provided online to learn more about the financial fundamentals required to become better investors.

Wal-Mart

When the late Sam Walton opened his first Wal-Mart store in 1962, company growth was his primary objec-

tive. In order to succeed he implemented all of the emerging technology available at the time. Over the years, his objective was achieved; Wal-Mart became the number 1 retailer in the world employing over 1,140,000 employees in almost 4,000 stores. Although the road to success has been phenomenal, it has not been without a few bumps along the way. During the mid-1990s, for example, the retailer experienced inventory problems and a sales slump. According to some analysts, it almost seemed like the retail giant lost its competitive edge. Corporate executives investigating the problem discovered that both managers and employees were not as technology-literate as they should be. They also discovered that just because the technology had been made available, it didn't mean that the managers and employees were using it. To remedy the problem both managers and employees received advanced training which eventually enabled Wal-Mart to correct problems and increase sales. Today, the company owns an elite information system which can automatically transmit data via satellite to all stores and corporate headquarters. Inventory is no longer an issue; suppliers are connected to the network and receive orders immediately. Wal-Mart recently expanded its network by adding an online ordering system for consumers. Wal-Mart.com is a virtual store and a complete companion to its physical stores.

E-Business: A Career Perspective

Companies who have the willingness to make the e-business conversion create extraordinary opportunities and have incredible advantages over their competitors. And while it's obvious e-business is here to stay, the largest stumbling block for companies using improved technology is not purchasing the new equipment, but training people or finding people who can use it. Today, companies are looking for employees who have the computer skills required to not only use new technology, but also improve on existing technology. In fact, many employers believe skilled talent is indispensable. Excellent jobs are available for those who have a vision on how to use improved technology.

- *Learning objectives* appear at the beginning of each chapter. All objectives signal important concepts to be mastered within the chapter.
- *Inside Business* is a chapter-opening case that highlights how successful companies do business on a day-to-day basis. These short cases were chosen to illustrate the key concepts and ideas described in each chapter.
- *Margin notes* are used throughout the text to reinforce both learning objectives and key terms.
- *Boxed features* highlight ethical behavior, change in the workplace, global issues, and the impact of technology. In addition, a boxed feature entitled Exploring Business highlights a wide range of contemporary business issues.

- *Spotlight* features highlight interesting facts about business and society and often provide a real-world example of an important concept within a chapter.
- *Using the Internet* features provide useful web addresses that relate to chapter material.
- *End-of-chapter materials* provide questions about the opening case, a chapter summary, a list of key terms, review and discussion questions, and a video case. The last section of every chapter is entitled Building Skills for Career Success and includes exercises devoted to exploring the Internet, developing critical thinking skills, building team skills, researching different careers, and improving communication skills.

In addition to the text, a number of student supplements will help you explore the world of business. We're especially proud of two items that are available with this edition of *Business*. The set of student CDs packaged with every new text purchased through your college bookstore will help you review important concepts with audio material that you can use at your convenience. We're also proud of the web site that accompanies this edition. Here you will find a computerized study guide, along with many other tools designed to help ensure your success in this course. If you want to take a look at the Internet support materials available for this edition of *Business,* go to: www.cengage.com/college/business and click on Text Web Sites.

As authors, we realize that you are our customers. We want you to be successful. And we want you to appreciate business and how it affects your life as an employee and a consumer. Since a text should always be evaluated by the students and instructors who use it, we would welcome and sincerely appreciate your comments and suggestions. Please feel free to contact us by using one of the following e-mail addresses:

Bill Pride	w-pride@tamu.edu
Bob Hughes	rjh8410@dcccd.edu
Jack Kapoor	kapoorj@cdnet.cod.edu

Business: A Definition

Business is the organized effort of individuals to produce and sell, for a profit, the goods and services that satisfy society's needs. The general term *business* refers to all such efforts within a society (as in "American business") or within an industry (as in "the steel business"). However, *a business* is a particular organization, such as Dudley Products, Inc., American Airlines, Inc., or Cracker Barrel Old Country Stores. To be successful, a business must perform three activities. It must be organized. It must satisfy needs. And it must earn a profit.

The Organized Effort of Individuals

For a business to be organized, it must combine four kinds of resources: material, human, financial, and informational. *Material* resources include the raw materials used in manufacturing processes, as well as buildings and machinery. For example, Sara Lee Corporation needs flour, sugar, butter, eggs, and other raw materials to produce the food products it sells worldwide. In addition, this Chicago-based company needs human, financial, and informational resources. *Human* resources are the people who furnish their labor to the business in return for wages. The *financial* resource is the money required to pay employees, purchase materials, and generally keep the business operating. And *information* is the resource that tells the managers of the business how effectively the other resources are being combined and used (see Figure 1.1).

Today, businesses are usually classified as one of three specific types. *Manufacturing businesses* are organized to process various materials into tangible goods, such as delivery trucks or towels. For example, Intel produces computer chips that are in turn sold to companies that manufacture computers. *Service businesses*

LEARNING OBJECTIVE

2 Define *business* and identify potential risks and rewards.

business the organized effort of individuals to produce and sell, for a profit, the goods and services that satisfy society's needs

10

figure 1.1

Combining Resources
A business must effectively combine all four resources to be successful.

Human resources → BUSINESS ← Informational resources

Material resources → ← Financial resources

produce services, such as haircuts, legal advice, or tax preparation. And some firms—called *marketing intermediaries*—are organized to buy products from manufacturers and then resell them. Sony Corporation is a manufacturer that produces stereo equipment, among other things. These products may be sold to a marketing intermediary such as Kmart Corporation, which then resells them to consumers in its retail stores. **Consumers** are individuals who purchase goods or services for their own personal use.

consumers individuals who purchase goods or services for their own personal use

Satisfying Needs

The ultimate objective of every firm must be to satisfy the needs of its customers. People generally don't buy goods and services simply to own them; they buy products and services to satisfy particular needs. People rarely buy an automobile solely to store it in a garage; they do, however, buy automobiles to satisfy their need for transportation. Some of us may feel this need is best satisfied by an air-conditioned BMW with stereo compact-disc player, automatic transmission, power seats and windows, and remote-control side mirrors. Others may believe a Ford Focus with a stick shift and an AM radio will do just fine. Both products are available to those who want them, along with a wide variety of other products that satisfy the need for transportation. To satisfy their customers' needs for information, Ford has joined up with Microsoft's *Carpoint* web site http://carpoint.msn.com/home/New.asp to help consumers find decision-critical information about their products and dealers from the comfort, convenience, and privacy of their own homes and offices. Ford and Microsoft hope to transform the site into a complete build-to-order system that will link customer orders for options directly with their supplier system. This way, customers get the products they want and Ford reduces the risks associated with guessing the inventories of cars its dealers should stock.[5]

And you think you've got books! For a company like Amazon.com, books are a way of life. In this warehouse facility, employees process orders and ship books to satisfy customers' needs.

When firms lose sight of their customers' needs they are likely to find the going rough. But when businesses understand their customers' needs and work to satisfy those needs, they are usually successful. Arkansas-based Wal-Mart Stores, Inc., provides the products its customers want and offers excellent prices. This highly successful discount-store organization continues to open new stores in the United States, Argentina, Brazil, Canada, China, Germany, and Mexico.

11

figure 1.2

The Relationship Between Sales Revenue and Profit
Profit is what remains after all business expenses have been deducted from sales revenue.

Business Profit

A business receives money (sales revenue) from its customers in exchange for goods or services. It must also pay out money to cover the expenses involved in doing business. If the firm's sales revenue is greater than its expenses, it has earned a profit. More specifically, as shown in Figure 1.2, **profit** is what remains after all business expenses have been deducted from sales revenue. (A negative profit, which results when a firm's expenses are greater than its sales revenue, is called a *loss*.)

The profit earned by a business becomes the property of its owners. So in one sense, profit is the reward business owners receive for producing goods and services that consumers want.

Profit is also the payment that business owners receive for assuming the considerable risks of ownership. One of these is the risk of not being paid. Everyone else—employees, suppliers, and lenders—must be paid before the owners. A second risk that owners run is the risk of losing whatever they have invested into the business. A business that cannot earn a profit is very likely to fail, in which case the owners lose whatever money, effort, and time they have invested. Internet-based book and CD retailer Amazon.com Inc. currently spends over $115 million each month to keep the company on track toward the eventual day when the firm will sell enough merchandise to generate profits for its shareholders. To date, Amazon's six years of operating losses total more than $1.2 billion, scaring away some who fear the firm will never reach the promised profit goals set by visionary founder Steve Bezos.[6] When a business is profitable, some businesses choose to give back a portion of their profits to the communities they serve. For information on how three different companies help children, read the Examining Ethics boxed feature.

To satisfy society's needs, and make a profit, a business must operate within the parameters of a nation's economic system. In the next section, we describe two different types of economic systems and how they affect not only businesses but also the people within a nation.

profit what remains after all business expenses have been deducted from sales revenue

LEARNING OBJECTIVE

3 Describe the two types of economic systems: capitalism and command economy.

Types of Economic Systems

Economics is the study of how wealth is created and distributed. By *wealth* we mean anything of value, including the products produced and sold by business. *How wealth is distributed* simply means "who gets what." The way in which people deal with the creation and distribution of wealth determines the kind of economic system, or **economy,** that a nation has.

Over the years, the economic systems of the world have differed in essentially two ways: (1) the ownership of the factors of production and (2) how they answer four basic economic questions that direct a nation's economic activity. **Factors of production** are the resources used to produce goods and services. There are four such factors:

- *Natural resources*—elements in their natural state that can be used in the production process. Typical examples include crude oil, forests, minerals, land, water, and even air.

economics the study of how wealth is created and distributed

economy the system through which a society answers the two economic questions—how wealth is created and distributed

factors of production natural resources, labor, capital, and entrepreneurship

- *Labor*—human resources such as managers and workers.
- *Capital*—money, facilities, equipment, and machines used in the operation of organizations. While most people think of capital as just money, it can also be the manufacturing equipment on a Ford automobile assembly line or a computer used in the corporate offices of Ace Hardware.
- *Entrepreneurship*—the willingness to take risks and the knowledge and ability to use the other factors of production efficiently. An **entrepreneur** is a person who risks his or her time, effort, and money to start and operate a business.

A nation's economic system significantly affects all the economic activities of its citizens and organizations. This far-reaching impact becomes more apparent when we consider that a country's economic system provides answers to four basic economic questions.

1. What goods and services—and how much of each—will be produced?
2. How will these goods and services be produced?
3. For whom will these goods and services be produced?
4. Who owns and who controls the major factors of production?

Capitalism

Capitalism is an economic system in which individuals own and operate the majority of businesses that provide goods and services. Capitalism stems from the theories of the eighteenth-century Scottish economist Adam Smith. In his book *Wealth of Nations*, published in 1776, Smith argued that a society's interests are best served when the individuals within that society are allowed to pursue their own self-interest.

Adam Smith's laissez-faire capitalism is based on four fundamental issues. First, Smith argued that the creation of wealth is properly the concern of private individuals, not of government. Second, the resources used to create wealth must be owned by private individuals. Smith argued that the owners of resources should be free to determine how these resources are used. They should also be free to enjoy the income, profits, and other benefits they might derive from the ownership of these resources. Third, Smith contended that economic freedom ensures the existence of competitive markets that allow both sellers and buyers to enter and exit as they choose. This freedom to enter or leave a market at will has given rise to the term *market economy*. A **market economy** (sometimes referred to as a *free-market economy*) is an economic system in which businesses and individuals make the decisions about what to produce and what to buy, and the market determines how much is sold and at what prices. Finally, in Smith's view, the role of government should be limited to providing defense against foreign enemies, ensuring internal order, and furnishing public works and education. With regard to the economy, government should act only as rule maker and umpire.

In other words, Smith believed that each person should be allowed to work toward his or her *own* economic gain, without interference from government. The French term *laissez faire* describes Smith's capitalistic system and implies that there shall be no interference in the economy. Loosely translated, it means "let them do" (as they see fit).

Capitalism in the United States

Our economic system is rooted in the laissez-faire capitalism of Adam Smith. However, our real-world economy is not as "laissez faire" as Smith would have liked because government participates as more than umpire and rule maker. Ours is, in fact, a **mixed economy,** one that exhibits elements of both capitalism and socialism.

entrepreneur a person who risks time, effort, and money to start and operate a business

capitalism an economic system in which individuals own and operate the majority of businesses that provide goods and services

market economy an economic system in which businesses and individuals decide what to produce and buy, and the market determines quantities sold and prices

mixed economy an economy that exhibits elements of both capitalism and socialism

Saturn: A true success story. There are no guarantees that Saturn will be successful just because it operates in a capitalistic society. However, companies like Saturn that produce goods and services that customers *really* want have a much better chance of being successful.

14

In today's economy, the four basic economic questions discussed at the beginning of this section of Chapter 1 are answered through the interaction of households, businesses, and governments. The interactions among these three groups are shown in Figure 1.3.

Households Households are consumers of goods and services, as well as owners of some of the factors of production. As *resource owners,* the members of households provide businesses with labor, land, buildings, and capital. In return, businesses pay wages, rent, and dividends and interest, which households receive as income.

As *consumers,* household members use their income to purchase the goods and services produced by business. Today almost two-thirds of our nation's total production consists of **consumer products:** goods and services purchased by individuals for personal consumption. (The remaining one-third is purchased by businesses and governments.) This means that consumers, as a group, are the biggest customer of American business.

consumer products goods and services purchased by individuals for personal consumption

Businesses Like households, businesses are engaged in two different exchanges. They exchange money for resources and use these resources to produce goods and services. Then they exchange their goods and services for sales revenue. This sales revenue, in turn, is exchanged for additional resources, which are used to produce and sell more goods and services. So the circular flow of Figure 1.3 is continuous.

Along the way, of course, business owners would like to remove something from the circular flow in the form of profits. And households try to retain some income as savings. But are profits and savings really removed from the flow? Usually not! When the economy is running smoothly, households are willing to invest their savings in businesses. They can do so directly, by buying ownership shares in businesses or by lending money to businesses. They can also invest indirectly, by placing their savings in bank accounts; banks then invest these savings as part of their normal business operations. In either case, savings usually find their way back into the circular flow in order to finance business activities.

figure 1.3

The Circular Flow in Our Modified Capitalist System
Our economic system is guided by the interaction of buyers and sellers, with the role of government being taken into account.

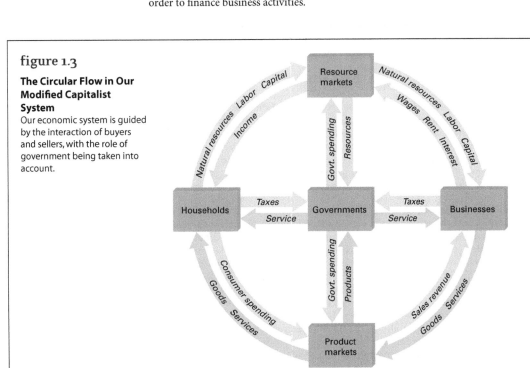

When business profits are distributed to business owners, these profits become household income. (Business owners are, after all, members of households.) And, as we saw, household income is retained in the circular flow as either consumer spending or invested savings. So business profits, too, are retained in the business system, and the circular flow is complete. How, then, does government fit in?

Governments   The framers of our Constitution desired as little government interference with business as possible. At the same time, the Preamble to the Constitution sets forth the responsibility of government to protect and promote the public welfare. Local, state, and federal governments discharge this responsibility through regulation and the provision of services. Government regulations of business are discussed in detail in various chapters of this book. The numerous services are important but either (1) would not be produced by private business firms or (2) would be produced only for those who could afford them. Typical services include national defense, police and fire protection, education, and construction of roads and highways. To pay for all these services, governments collect a variety of taxes from households (such as personal income taxes and sales taxes) and from businesses (corporate income taxes).

Figure 1.3 shows this exchange of taxes for government services. It also shows government spending of tax dollars for resources and products required to provide these services. In other words, governments, too, return their incomes to the business system through the resource and product markets.

Actually, with government included, our circular flow looks more like a combination of several flows. And in reality it is. The important point is that, together, the various flows make up a single unit—a complete economic system that effectively provides answers to the basic economic questions. Simply put, the system works.

spotLight

Source: Copyright 2000, USA TODAY. Reprinted with permission.

Command Economies

Before we discuss how to measure a nation's economic performance, we look quickly at another economic system called a command economy. A **command economy** is an economic system in which the government decides what goods and services will be produced, how they will be produced, who gets available goods and services, and what prices will be charged. The answers to all four basic economic questions are determined, at least to some degree, through centralized government planning. Today, two types of economic systems—*socialism* and *communism*—serve as examples of command economies.

command economy an economic system in which the government decides what will be produced, how it will be produced, who gets what is produced, and the prices of what is produced

Socialism   In a *socialist* economy, the key industries are owned and controlled by the government. Such industries usually include transportation, utilities, communications, banking, and industries producing important materials such as steel. Land, buildings, and raw materials may also be the property of the state in a socialist economy. Depending on the country, private ownership of smaller businesses is permitted to varying degrees. People usually may choose their own occupations, but many work in state-owned industries.

What to produce and how to produce it are determined in accordance with national goals, which are based on projected needs and the availability of resources—at least for government-owned industries. The distribution of goods and services—who gets what—is also controlled by the state to the extent that it controls rents and wages. Among the professed aims of socialist countries are the equitable distribution of income, the elimination of poverty, the distribution of social services (such as medical care) to all who need them, and elimination of the economic waste that supposedly accompanies capitalistic competition.

16

Part I The Environment of Business

Britain, France, Sweden, and India are democratic countries whose economies include a very visible degree of socialism. Other, more authoritarian countries may actually have socialist economies; however, we tend to think of them as communist because of their almost total lack of freedom.

Communism If Adam Smith was the father of capitalism, Karl Marx was the father of communism. In his writings during the mid-nineteenth century, Marx advocated a classless society whose citizens together owned all economic resources. All workers would then contribute to this *communist* society according to their ability and would receive benefits according to their need.

Since the breakup of the Soviet Union and economic reforms in China and most of the eastern European countries, the best remaining examples of communism are North Korea and Cuba. Today these so-called communist economies seem to practice a strictly controlled kind of socialism. Almost all economic resources are owned by the government. The basic economic questions are answered through centralized state planning, which sets prices and wages as well. In this planning, the needs of the state generally outweigh the needs of individual citizens. Emphasis is placed on the production of goods the government needs rather than on the products that consumers might want, so there are frequent shortages of consumer goods. Workers have little choice of jobs, but special skills or talents seem to be rewarded with special privileges. Various groups of professionals (bureaucrats, university professors, and athletes, for example) fare much better than, say, factory workers.

4. Which of the following is an accurate conclusion based on the "Job Boom" visual aid?

   a. The federal government predicts that the computer industry will have the highest percentage of increase in employees.

   b. Federal projections indicate that the computer and health services industries will add about the same number of jobs.

   c. According to federal projections, the residential maintenance industry will grow faster than any other industry.

   d. The federal government says that the residential maintenance industry will grow much faster than the health services industry.

5. On the blanks provided, write a brief definition for each of the following key terms:

   free enterprise: _____

   e-business: _____

   business: _____

   consumers: _____

   profit: _____

6. Describe the four resources that must be combined to organize and operate a business. How do they differ from the economist's factors of production?

_____

_____

_____

_____

_____

7. What are the four basic economic questions? How are they answered in a capitalist economy?

_____

_____

_____

_____

_____

8. Describe the four fundamental issues required for a laissez-faire capitalist economy.

_____

_____

_____

_____

_____

9. Why is the American economy called a mixed economy?

_____

_____

_____

_____

_____

10. Based on Figure 1.3 in the preceding section of the business chapter, outline the economic interactions between government and businesses in our business system. Outline those between government and households.

   _____

   _____

   _____

   _____

   _____

11. How does capitalism differ from socialism and communism?

   _____

   _____

   _____

   _____

   _____